BORN OF THE EUCHARIST

Halfway through *Born of the Eucharist: A Spirituality for Priests* an image came clearly to me, a memory, of a *panificio*, an Italian bakery. Just passing by, you are surrounded by the aroma of bread baking. Then, as you walk in, there are big baskets of several kinds of bread, of various shapes and different sizes—round, elongated, flat, and in several shades of tan.

The flavors, consistency, and crusts are multiple, some slightly sweet, others tending to a sour or a more salty palate; some soft, others crunchy. All make my mouth water, yet each of them is that same basic food—bread—beautiful, tasty, and nutritious.

So too is this book, a rich and varied collection of essays of different lengths and approaches. They range from theological and scriptural reflections like those of Cardinals Avery Dulles, S.J., and Albert Vanhoye, S.J., to deep and more experience-based meditations like the beautiful writing by Fr. Gabriel O'Donnell, O.P. In addition, there are *panini*—small breads of one or a few pages—that catch and share a specific aspect of the "bread of life" in the life of the priest.

Msgr. Stephen Rossetti, who also contributes a few deep and personal reflections, is the chief baker, who has compiled a healthy book for the hungry priest. Young men in discernment will likewise experience an increased hunger for the priesthood. Finally, Catholics who seek to learn about the dynamic relationship between the Eucharist and the priest will be nourished, enlightened, and uplifted by reading this book.

Fr. Italo Dell'Oro, C.R.S.
Director, Ministry to Priests
Archdiocese of Galveston-Houston

From the hearts and minds of shepherds—well known and not— here is a lively gathering of eucharistic wisdom that renders priesthood freshly palpable. Clearly, the priests and bishops who come together in this volume to witness to the power of the presence of the Lord in the Eucharist in their lives, draw their strength and joy from this most blessed of sacraments. Born of the Eucharist is a real opportunity for each of us priests to return to the Lord's Table, the source of our vocation, and be renewed in the joy. Msgr. Stephen Rossetti serves his brother priests very well in hosting this gathering.

Rev. Raymond P. Roden, PsyD
Vicariate for Clergy and Consecrated Life
Diocese of Brooklyn

BORN OF THE EUCHARIST

A SPIRITUALITY *for* PRIESTS

With a Reflection by Cardinal Avery Dulles, S.J.

Edited by

STEPHEN J. ROSSETTI

Author of *The Joy of Priesthood*

ave maria press AMP notre dame, indiana

Nihil Obstat: Rev. Darr Schoenhofen
Imprimatur: Most Rev. Robert J. Cunningham
Bishop of the Diocese of Syracuse
Given at Syracuse, NY on June 12, 2009

Founded in 1865, Ave Maria Press is a ministry of the Indiana Province of Holy Cross.

www.avemariapress.com

ISBN-10: 1-59471-217-4   ISBN 13: 978-1-59471-217-3

Cover image © Réunion des Musées Nationaux / Art Resource, NY

Cover and text design by John R. Carson.

Printed and bound in the United States of America.

Library of Congress Cataloging-in-Publication Data
Born of the Eucharist : a spirituality for priests / edited by Stephen J. Rossetti.
   p. cm.
   Includes bibliographical references.
   ISBN-13: 978-1-59471-217-3 (pbk.)
   ISBN-10: 1-59471-217-4 (pbk.)
   1. Lord's Supper--Catholic Church. 2. Priesthood--Catholic Church. 3. Pastoral theology--Catholic Church. I. Rossetti, Stephen J., 1951-
   BX2215.3.B67 2009
   234'.163--dc22
                                        2009019527

This book is dedicated to
Cardinal Avery Dulles, S.J.
August 24, 1918–December 12, 2008
Faithful Jesuit, Master Theologian, Man of the Church,
Dedicated Teacher, Humble Man, Lover of Christ.

Your many students and friends thank you.

🙢

At the Last Supper, we were born as priests.
—John Paul II
Holy Thursday Letter, 2004

The more intensely he lives in Christ,
the more authentically he can celebrate the Eucharist.
The Eucharist is at the heart of the priest's spirituality.
—John Paul II
General Audience, June 9, 1993

CONTENTS

INTRODUCTION
Rev. Msgr. Stephen J. Rossetti

———

When you read through the eight chapters and twenty-one reflections by these exemplary priests and bishops, you will find many interesting thoughts, ideas, stories, and experiences. While they are engaging and enlightening in themselves, there is a "buried treasure" underneath it all. The treasure lies in the dynamic personal relationship of these fine priests to the Eucharist. The intensity and profundity of this relationship witnesses to us most powerfully.

Down through the centuries, there have been many writings that wax eloquently about the relationship of the Eucharist and the priest. These are important. But it is the lived experience of our priests today that speaks all the more poignantly. In his essay, Cardinal Avery Dulles, reflecting on the priesthood and the Eucharist, wrote, "This is our lofty calling, than which, I think, there can be no higher." Cardinal Francis George, in his contribution, shared a moment during a papal Mass when he "had a profound experience of the unity in Christ." Msgr. Paul Lenz wrote about attending a Mass with Padre Pio in which he "felt seized and transported by grace." Fr. David Toups related an experience on retreat, holding the host in his hands and with tears in his eyes when he knew that, "I was holding

> *In a very real way, the renewal of the Church is linked to the renewal of the priesthood.*
> —*John Paul II*

1

the pearl of great price, Jesus Christ." Fr. Gabriel O'Donnell opened his reflections with: "The Eucharist has always been the center of my life."

While the Second Vatican Council and a plethora of other Church documents rightly speak of the centrality of the Eucharist, we see these truths come alive in the inspiring witnesses of our authors. There seems to emerge from these pages and the various authors, when one listens most deeply, a "single voice" that points to the altar and cries out with John the Baptist, "Look, there is the lamb of God who takes away the sins of the world!"

The greatest witness to the truths of our faith has always been the living faith of believers. And a great witness to the health, vibrancy, and, in truth, sanctity of our priests and bishops today is their love of the Eucharist, and thus, their love of Christ. When we read the words written from the hearts of these men, it fills us with a great hope.

IDENTITY OF PRIESTHOOD AND EUCHARIST

This univocal witness to the centrality of the Eucharist and to its real presence of Christ strongly affirms the Church's consistent teaching about the connection of priesthood and Eucharist. The Eucharist is not simply one function of the priest, not merely one task among many that he endeavors to perform with reverence. The connection is deeper and more profound.

Every great reform has in some way been linked to the rediscovery of belief in the Lord's eucharistic presence among the people.
—Sacramentum Caritatis 6

John Paul II, in his personal letter to priests on Holy Thursday 2004, told his brothers, "The ministerial priesthood . . . is born, lives and works and bears fruit 'de Eucharistia.'" This is a powerful statement: *we are born of the Eucharist.* It is out of the very essence of the Eucharist that priesthood comes into being. It is no accident that we celebrate both the institution of the Eucharist and the ministerial priesthood on the same night, Holy Thursday. The priesthood and the Eucharist are interwoven and share a common identity. John Paul II put it succinctly when he said, "There is no priesthood without the Eucharist and no Eucharist without the priesthood."[1]

It is little wonder, then, that the priestly authors of this book each have a profound connection to the Eucharist. These authors have presided at Mass thousands of times. Again and again and again, they have ascended to the altar and offered the Holy Sacrifice. One might think, given a certain secular perspective, that such a repetitious act could become routine, blasé, perhaps even boring. But such is not the case. Clearly, the Eucharist has steadily grown in meaning and centrality in their lives. Each of them continues to plumb, ever more deeply, this wellspring of Christian life. And so should we.

EUCHARISTIC REFORM OF THE PRIESTHOOD

Shortly before his death, John Paul II called for a renewal of the Church and said it was "urgently needed."[2] He later added that this renewal must be accompanied by a renewal of the clergy: "In a very real way, the renewal of the Church is linked to the renewal of the priesthood."[3] I believe these words are true for us today and that we are in the midst of a graced time of renewal.

I believe that this call to renewal is not to take a priesthood that has become *bad* and to make it *good* again. Rather, it is to take the *good* priesthood of today and to fill it full of *saints*. There are many signs of life and health in our priesthood today. There are tens of thousands of priests who toil tirelessly and truly heroically each day. They are continuing to show us the ordinary means to faithfulness and, at times, even to sanctity. They will be the key to a renewal of the Church. As St. John Vianney said to his bishop, "If you wish to convert your diocese you must make all your parish priests saints."[4]

These are not ordinary times; the call for a renewal is especially urgent. Atheism is spreading, particularly in some of the wealthier nations. The Church in these areas is increasingly ignored or persecuted in modern, middle-class ways. In our Internet world with its hyper-connectivity, I believe that atheism will spread steadily across the globe.

Militantly atheistic spokespersons such as Christopher Hitchens (author of *God Is Not Great*) or Richard Dawkins *(The God Delusion)* unabashedly and loudly proclaim that there is no God and there is no next life. "Christianity," as I heard Mr. Hitchens say in a lecture in London, "is evil rubbish."

Perhaps more dangerous are the increasing millions who nominally profess some Christianity or a belief in God, but who live their lives completely as if there is no God. I have come to recognize that this, too, is really a form of atheism, albeit a functional one. We are, in many of the richest nations of the world, being enveloped by atheism, explicit or functional, but atheism nonetheless. And it will spread.

> There is a particular interplay between the Eucharist and the priesthood, an interplay which goes back to the Upper Room: these two sacraments were born together and their destiny is indissolubly linked until the end of the world.
> —John Paul II, Holy Thursday letter, 2004

It is time for us in the Church to move beyond our tendency toward breast-beating and excessive self-introspection that, at times, threatens to paralyze us. We ought never to be embarrassed or hesitant about explaining the cause of our hope. We ought to move forward and preach with the confidence that comes from Jesus Christ. Jesus himself spoke with an authority that often amazed his hearers: "the crowds were astonished at his teaching, for he taught them as one having authority" (Mt 7:28–29).

Our renewed spreading of the gospel, the New Evangelization, will necessarily be led by a host of holy priests and bishops filled with the power, authority, and confidence of the eucharistic Christ. As Pope Benedict has said in *Sacramentum Caritatis*, "Every great reform has in some way been linked to the rediscovery of belief in the Lord's eucharistic presence among his people" (*S Car* 6). It is my hope and prayer that the witness of these authors will enkindle in many a deeper understanding, thirst, and love for Christ in the Eucharist. Empowered by this indwelling Christ, we cannot but proclaim true Hope and true Light to a darkening world.

Miracles Before the Eucharist
Archbishop Timothy M. Dolan

On June 24, 2002, I arrived in Milwaukee on the day before the public announcement that I had been appointed as tenth archbishop of Milwaukee. I was a nervous wreck. I had a big job ahead of me, in an archdiocese I knew little about, in the midst of a time of national scandal, to follow a very prominent and long-serving archbishop.

But what made me most apprehensive was the prospect of meeting my predecessor. Archbishop Rembert Weakland had a national, actually international, stature; he had just resigned after acknowledging and apologizing for past sins; and, although I hardly knew him, word on the street was that we came from different "theological backgrounds," which is a euphemistic way of saying that he was looked upon as a "liberal," I as a "conservative."

Because the loaf of bread is one, we, though many, are one body, for we all partake of the one loaf.
—1 Corinthians 10:17

His gracious hospitality that evening, substantive conversation, candid assessment of the challenges awaiting me, and his assurances of ongoing support, made me feel very welcome, and softened considerably the nervousness I was experiencing. But, what really gave me peace and confidence came early the next morning.

I couldn't sleep, and I was anticipating controversial questions at the press conference. Plus, I was still unsure about how my predecessor and I would get along. By 4:00 a.m. I gave up on sleep. I got out of bed, showered, dressed, grabbed my breviary, and made my way, at about 4:45 in the morning, to the little chapel downstairs . . . and there sat Rembert Weakland, with his breviary, before the Blessed Sacrament in the tabernacle. My fears evaporated. Between the two of us was a difference in age of twenty-five years, in weight of about sixty pounds, a variation of theological outlook probably. But it was suddenly and dramatically evident to me that we were *one* in our faith, our priestly vocation, our apostolic bond, our prayer, and our trust in Jesus, really and truly present in the Most Blessed Sacrament.

> If you want the faithful who are entrusted to your care to pray willingly and well, you must give them an example and let them see you praying in church. A priest kneeling devoutly and reverently before the tabernacle, and pouring forth prayers to God with all his heart, is a wonderful example to the Christian people and serves as an inspiration.
> —*Sacerdotii Nostri Primordia* 49

I propose to you that this was a *miracle*. Jesus was saying to me, as he had said to his first priests and bishops, his apostles, "Do not be afraid." This miracle occurred before the eucharistic presence of Christ. Miracles often occur before the Eucharist. The Eucharist itself is a miracle.

As rector of the North American College, I had the joy of reading the autobiographies of over three hundred men requesting admission. Never was I unmoved by those personal testimonies. Very often, those promising young men had discerned a vocation to the priesthood while in silent prayer before Jesus in the Eucharist. Many vividly recalled how Jesus, in the Blessed Sacrament, had transformed their fears into trust, their doubts into hope. It's not that any of them had audibly heard the voice of Christ—I would have reread their "psychologicals" had that been the case! No—but, in the stillness of their souls, conscious of the real presence, they had sensed him whispering, "Come, follow me!"

Each Sunday, I have the joy of celebrating 8:00 a.m. Mass at our cathedral. After Mass once, a woman said, "You do something that really inspires me!" I wanted to kiss her, since compliments are rare these days. My conceited side kicked in as I began to anticipate what she would praise me for: a sterling sermon? A new diocesan initiative? A witty comment to a crabby reporter? "I am so inspired," she continued, "that I see you before the tabernacle every Sunday before Mass." I'll be. . . . Of course, I hardly do that to impress her, or anybody. I do it because I need miracles.

Priest and Eucharist: No Higher Calling

Cardinal Avery Dulles, S.J.*

In these days of diminishing numbers of priestly ordinations and ever-increasing accountability, priests who are engaged in parish work must, I suppose, feel pulled apart by conflicting claims on their time and energies. Theirs is probably more the lot of Martha than of Mary. After all, they are, very likely, managers of a large plant. They have a parish church and no doubt a rectory and possibly a school, a convent, or other buildings to maintain; they have employees who have problems *Priesthood is more a matter of being than of doing.* about working conditions, wages, and hours; they have educational programs, such as CCD and RCIA; they have endless rounds of committee meetings, Baptisms, marriage preparations, weddings, sick calls, and funerals. Priests are called upon to hear confessions and to make time for spiritual counseling. They have the Liturgy of the Hours to say daily, and they strive to find time for personal prayer. Priests have to maintain relationships with other priests, with their bishops or religious superiors, with friends and family. And they have to take care of their personal needs, including shopping,

*This paper, originally given as a Day of Recollection for priests in Dunwoodie, New York, March 9, 2005, was personally given by Cardinal Dulles for this book and has been edited for this use.

doctor's appointments, and time for relaxation. As an aca-demic, I do not experience all the pressures that are upon them, but I think I understand some of the demands that they must feel.

And yet, as Jesus told the sisters of Lazarus, only one thing is necessary. We all have to find what is truly central in our lives, and let it dictate the priorities. The all-important question for us may be: Who am I as a priest?

PRIESTHOOD AND EUCHARIST ARE PROFOUNDLY INTERCONNECTED

I like to think that priesthood is more a matter of being than of doing. At ordination, the priest receives an indelible mark that makes him different—"ontologically" different, some prefer to say—no matter whether he does anything or not. Even if he performed no priestly ministry, he would still be a priest forever. But, of course, he should not be idle. He is ordained in order to perform a specific service toward the Lord and toward the people of God.

The essence of priestly service has perhaps never been better expressed than by the Letter to the Hebrews, which tells us:

> Every high priest is taken from among men and made their representative before God, to offer gifts and sacrifices for sins. For this reason, he is bound to offer sacrifice for his own sins as well as for those of the people. And one does not take the honor upon himself, but is called by God, just as Aaron was. (Heb 5:1, 3–4)

The priest is a mediator; he offers sacrifices to God on behalf of himself and the people, and in return he distributes to the people the gifts that come from God. Thus, we may include in the notion of priesthood the vocation to be, in the phrase of St. Paul, "stewards of the mysteries of God" (1 Cor 4:1).

To pray, to offer sacrifice, and to distribute to the community the heavenly gifts that God is pleased to bestow: this is our lofty calling, than which, I think, there can be no higher. This mediatory task, both upward and downward, must be the hinge on which our life turns, the source of our inner peace, and the unifying element that determines the apportionment of our activities.

There were certain priorities in the mediating work of Jesus himself. Conscious that he had come into the world to offer his body in obedience to God (cf. Heb 10:5–10), he hastened with a certain impatience toward the passion at the appointed hour (cf. Jn 12:27). At the Last Supper he declared: "I have eagerly desired to eat this Passover with you before I suffer" (Lk 22:15). For, at that meal, he anticipated the sacrifice he was to offer on Calvary and distributed its fruits to his faithful disciples, commissioning them to perform the same rite in memory of him.

> The Church is vivified and held in unity by this supreme sacrament.

The Last Supper was the moment when Jesus instituted the new covenant and commissioned the Twelve to be the principal bearers and ministers of that covenant. He might have instituted the new covenant in some other way, as the covenants with Abraham, Noah, Moses, and David had been instituted. But as a sign of the conviviality that characterizes the heavenly banquet, he opted for the form of a meal. Jesus is the host who both serves his guests and enters into table companionship with them.

The Last Supper is not just one more of the series of suppers that Jesus had been sharing with the disciples and others over the preceding months and years; it is a unique farewell meal in which Jesus bestowed his parting gift, his very self. At this point, he accomplished in actual fact what he had promised to do at Capharnaum, when he declared that his flesh was real food and his blood real drink (Jn 6:55), given "for the life of the world" (Jn 6:51). Under the external forms of bread and wine, he offers himself to sustain and nourish the Church in order to make it, in a true sense, his body. The Church is vivified and held in unity by this supreme sacrament.

Celebrated by the Church after the resurrection, the Eucharist "proclaims the death of the Lord until he comes." The Church continues to do what Jesus did at the Last Supper, but in a different manner. The Last Supper looked forward to, and enacted in advance, the sacrifice to come; the Eucharist points back to Calvary, and makes it present in new form.

In the ordination ritual, the ordaining prelate gives to the ordinand this charge: "The sacrifice of Christ will be offered sacramentally in an unbloody way through your hands. Understand the meaning of what you do; put into practice what you celebrate. When you recall the mystery of the death and resurrection of the Lord, strive to die to sin and to walk in the new life of Christ."

Every ordained priest participates in the threefold office of Christ. Because Christ was priest, prophet, and king, the Christian priesthood is not only cultic but also prophetic and royal. But because the cultic or sacerdotal function is primary, members of the presbyterate and episcopate are commonly called priests.

It would be possible but tedious to heap up an almost endless series of quotations from the Fathers and Doctors of the Church and from popes and councils to the effect that the supreme activity of the ministerial priest is to celebrate the Eucharist. At Vatican II, *Presbyterorum Ordinis* (Decree on the Life and Ministry of Priests) taught that it is in the eucharistic sacrifice that priests fulfill their highest office (*PO* 13). The same Decree goes on to say that the eucharistic sacrifice is "the center and root of the whole priestly life" (*PO* 14).

In the eucharistic sacrifice priests fulfill their highest office.

Similar statements can be found in several other texts of Vatican II, in the statement *De Sacerdotio Ministeriali* (On the Ministerial Priesthood) issued by the Synod of Bishops in 1971, and in the Directory for the Life and Ministry of Priests published by the Congregation for the Clergy in 1994 (48). Pope John Paul II believes the same with all his heart and has many times so declared. In his general audience on May 12, 1993, for example, he said: "I reaffirm with conviction and deep spiritual joy that the presbyter is above all a man of the Eucharist."[5] "The Eucharist," he writes in *Dominicae Cenae*, "is the *raison d'être* of the priesthood" (*DC* 2). So profoundly interconnected are the two, he states, that "there can be no Eucharist without the priesthood, just as there can be no priesthood without the Eucharist."[6] The Eucharist could not exist without us priests but, without the Eucharist, our existence as priests would be a lifeless shadow.[7]

EUCHARIST IS THE SACRAMENT OF SACRAMENTS

Theologians explain that the entire sacramental life of the Church revolves about the Eucharist, which is the center toward which all the sacraments converge and from which they radiate like the spokes of a wheel from the hub, like heat from a furnace, or like rays of light from a lamp. St. Thomas somewhere calls the Eucharist the sacrament of sacraments, the source and goal of all sacramental life.

The Eucharist is the very center of parish life.

Baptism and Confirmation bestow a mark or character enabling their recipients to take part as active participants in eucharistic worship and to receive Holy Communion. The sacraments of Penance and the Anointing of the Sick dispose the faithful to receive the sacrament worthily and fruitfully. The primary effect of ordination is to produce ministers capable of offering Holy Mass.

Matrimony is of all the sacraments most difficult to connect with the Eucharist, but I believe that a close connection can be found if we understand it as a covenant of mutual union, founded on the nuptial covenant between Christ and his Church. John Paul II in his apostolic exhortation on the family, *Familiaris Consortio,* writes:

> The Eucharist is the very source of Christian marriage. The Eucharistic Sacrifice, in fact, represents Christ's covenant of love with the Church, sealed with his blood on the cross. In this sacrifice of the New and Eternal Covenant, Christian spouses encounter the source from which their own marriage covenant flows, [by which it] is interiorly structured and continuously renewed. (57)

Not all ministry, to be sure, is sacramental. The parish has to have effective programs for education, for spiritual formation, and for evangelization. But all of these programs should be inspired by, and oriented toward, the Eucharist as the very center of parish life. The Sunday Mass, in particular, should be the culmination. It should be offered with dignity and at times with a certain solemnity, marked by beauty of language, music, gesture, and visual setting. It should be an occasion when the parish joyfully experiences its unity as a worshiping community, with the various ministers performing their proper functions, under the presidency of the priest-celebrant.

Pope John Paul II's apostolic letter *Dies Domini*, released on Pentecost Sunday 1998, recalls that the first sabbath commemorated in scripture is that of God himself, who paused after the labor of creation to contemplate the beauty of the world he had made.

Sunday Eucharist is an epiphany of the Church.

Each Sunday, Christians pause from the labors of the week to give praise to God for all that he has done, not only the gifts of creation but those of redemption, coming to a climax in Christ's resurrection from the dead and his entrance into his sabbath rest. The eighth day of the week coincides with the first day, expressing the arrival of the new age. It looks forward to the endless day when we and the whole Church will enter into the promised sabbath rest.

The day of the Lord, says the Pope, is also the day of the Church. The Sunday Eucharist is an epiphany of the Church as it gathers round the altar of the Lord in the presence of the bishop or the priest, who represents the bishop. Sunday observance, therefore, is the privileged place in which communion is proclaimed and nurtured, so that the Church may effectively perform her role as the sacrament of unity.

THE PRIEST'S ROLE IN THE EUCHARIST IS INDISPENSABLE

The Mass is made up of a call to worship, a penitential rite, prayers that express the community's needs, hopes, and gratitude, readings to instruct the faithful, a homily to expound the word of God, an offering of gifts, the Holy Sacrifice, Holy Communion, and the final blessing and dismissal. The priest plays an indispensable role at every stage of this liturgy. He is specially appointed to pray on behalf of the community, to proclaim the word of God, to consecrate the sacred species, and to feed the flock of Christ.

The Eucharist can never be the private worship of an individual or a club. It is always a public act of the Church as such. For this reason, its celebration requires a minister capable of linking the local community to the diocesan bishop and through him to the whole Catholic communion. Ordained by a bishop in the apostolic succession, the priest is also the bond that links the Eucharist vertically in time with what Jesus did for the apostles at the Last Supper. To underline the Catholic and apostolic dimensions of the sacrament, the missal includes commemorations of the local bishop, the Pope, and apostles, and selected saints and martyrs.

In some quarters, confusion and doubts have arisen concerning the role of the ordained priest in the Eucharist. Is it sufficient for him to pronounce the words of consecration, delegating everything else to members of the congregation? The "General Instruction" at the beginning of the Roman Missal takes pains to eliminate any such minimalism. It points out that the priest alone offers the gifts at the altar. He alone recites the Eucharistic Prayer, with the people responding according to the rubrics. Ordinarily, only those who are sacramentally ordained may preach at the Eucharist. They alone may break the consecrated hosts and pour the precious blood into the chalice. And they are the ordinary ministers of Holy Communion, with certain exceptions to be noted later.

Try earnestly to give the congregation something solid that will nourish them spiritually.

The readings from holy scripture and the ensuing homily are important parts of the Mass. The Second Vatican Council declares that "the liturgy of the word and the eucharistic liturgy are so closely bound together that they form a single act of worship"

(*SC* 56). Several times the Council speaks of the two tables—that of the word of God and that of the body of Christ—from which the Church receives the bread of life and hands them on to the faithful (*DV* 21; cf. *SC* 51). "For in the sacred books," says the Council, "the Father who is in heaven meets his children with great love and speaks with them; and the force and power in the word of God is so great that it remains the support and energy of the Church, the strength of faith for her sons, the food of the soul, the pure and perennial source of spiritual life" (*SC* 6).

The proclamation of the gospel, which is the high point of the Liturgy of the Word, is reserved by the Church's tradition to ordained ministers. The homily is ordinarily given by the priest celebrant himself, although it may be assigned on occasion to another priest or to a deacon.

In his apostolic letter on the *Dies Domini*, Pope John Paul II says that now, more than thirty years after the Council, "We need to assess how well the word of God is being proclaimed. . . . It is the duty of those who exercise the ministry of the word to prepare the reflection on the word of the Lord by prayer and study of the sacred text, so that they may then express its contents faithfully and apply them to people's concerns and to their daily lives" (*DD* 40). In the homily, the priest has a precious opportunity to instruct the people, bringing out the relationship of the inspired word to their circumstances, needs, and capacities. In these days when the Church has so little opportunity to mold the ideas and values of the faithful, these few minutes of instruction should not be wasted. We should try earnestly to give the congregation something solid that will nourish them spiritually, correct any unhealthy tendencies, warn the people against serious spiritual dangers, and build up their joy and confidence in their faith. In her seminary training, the Church tries to prepare her priests so that their homilies will strengthen the zeal of the congregants and enrich their understanding of the word of God. The priest must maintain a certain level of

Pray earnestly for the grace to make this offering from the heart.

intellectual and spiritual life in order to measure up to the demands of preaching, which can be quite stringent.

In preaching, the priest relies not only on his personal gifts but also on his power of orders and his faculties from the bishop so that he can speak, not simply in his own name, but officially, on behalf of the Church as such. In preaching, the priest shares in the magisterium of the teaching Church, though in a subordinate way, under the Pope and the bishops.

At the Offertory, the priest has the office of presenting to the Lord the gifts of the people, represented by the bread and wine. We who are priests should pray earnestly for the grace to make this offering from the heart, placing ourselves, as it were, on the paten and in the chalice which we lift up to the Lord, together with needs and intentions of all the people whom we serve.

At the consecration, the priest performs his supreme act, in the person of Christ the Lord. The priest is not alone in offering the sacrifice, but the people offer it with him and through his hands, so that his role is primary. He speaks the very words of Christ, in the first person singular, "This is my body. . . . This is my blood." There is no need for dramatics at this point; it is not a matter of play-acting, in which we try to create the illusion that we are Jesus Christ. No, we remain just what we were, but we let the grace of ordination work through us as we speak and act in the very person of Christ. As we proclaim

> It must never be forgotten that our reception of Baptism and Confirmation is ordered to the Eucharist. Accordingly, our pastoral practice should reflect a more unitary understanding of the process of Christian initiation . . . The Holy Eucharist, then, brings Christian initiation to completion and represents the centre and goal of all sacramental life.
> —*Sacramentum Caritatis* 17

the death of the Lord, he takes over without any special effort on our part. We simply lend him our voice and our hands, and he performs his ministry through us. Recognizing that our priesthood is simply a participation in that of Christ the High Priest, we let him draw us into his sacrificial action, begging him to configure our minds and hearts more perfectly to his.

The priest has the responsibility to unify the community around the altar, eliminating the individualistic detachment or the factionalism that can sometimes internally divide parishes or separate them from the larger Church. The sign of peace immediately preceding Holy Communion should not be an empty formality, but an expression of mutual love and reconciliation among the members of the congregation, symbolizing the unity of the universal Church to which they belong.

> It is not the power of man which makes what is put before us the body and blood of Christ, but the power of Christ himself who was crucified for us. The priest standing there in the place of Christ says these words but their power and grace are from God. "This is my body," he says, and these words transform what lies before him.
> —St. John Chrysostom, *Homilies on the Treachery of Judas* 1, 6

Holy Communion is a preeminent moment of the liturgical action. The celebrant and concelebrants first receive communion themselves, as is necessary for the sacrifice to reach completion. The priest, as I have said, is the ordinary minister of Holy Communion, although deacons may assist. In the event of real necessity where clergy are lacking, suitable lay persons may be designated as extraordinary ministers of Holy Communion.

The reception of Holy Communion, of course, is a sacred moment in which everyone who partakes, including the priest, should be left to his or her own thoughts. Some might wish to pray over the words of Jesus, "Behold, I stand at the door and knock" (Rev 3:20). He begs to be admitted into our hearts so that he may transform us with his love. We priests are privileged to feed our people with the Bread of Life, so that they may become, so to speak, a eucharistic people. The specific grace of this sacrament, according to Catholic tradition, is the unity of the Mystical Body, a unity of devotion, peace, and charity.

The missal contains very beautiful prayers before and after Communion, which afford splendid material for our meditation. I especially like the prayer that the priest is to say silently before the ablutions, "What we have received with our lips, O Lord, may we receive with a pure mind, and from being a passing gift may it become for us an everlasting remedy" (from the Latin).

As you may be aware, in 2002 the United States received an indult by way of experiment, permitting extraordinary ministers of Holy Communion to assist in the purification of the sacred vessels in cases of real need. Unless

The celebrant or the deacon commissions the congregation to bring gospel values into their daily lives.

this indult is promptly renewed, it will expire on March 22, 2005.[8] After that date only priests, deacons, and installed acolytes will be authorized to purify the chalice and paten. These and other liturgical norms should not be dismissed as meticulous rubrics dictated by a legalistic mentality. They are intended to protect the sacredness of the Eucharist and the integrity of the ministerial priesthood, which is intrinsically related to the Eucharist.

The conclusion of the Mass, with the final blessing and the dismissal, should not be simply a way of saying, "Thank God it's over, now we can go home." The priest should be conscious of the privilege of bestowing the blessing in the name of the triune God. In saying the *Ite, missa est* the celebrant or the deacon commissions the congregation to bring gospel values into their daily lives, including their home, their neighborhood, their business or profession. They are to be bearers of the message of Christ, evangelizing their particular environment by word and by example (cf. *Mane*

Nobiscum 24). It seems obvious in our time that the world stands in desperate need of being transformed by the message of the gospel. In the past, we have often failed to give our Catholic people a lively sense of mission. But, especially since Vatican II, the popes have been trying to overcome the complacency or fear or indifference, whatever it may be, that turns the Church so much in upon herself. Our role as priests is to communicate to the laity a greater realization of their responsibility to Christianize the world.

FOSTERING A EUCHARISTIC DEVOTION

A lively faith in the real and substantial presence of Christ in the Eucharist gives rise to a variety of eucharistic devotions beyond and outside the celebration of Mass. Catholic teaching has constantly defended reverence for the reserved sacrament. In the sixteenth century, the Council of Trent repudiated opinions to the effect that Christ was present only in the distribution of Holy Communion, or that reservation of the host was not legitimate except for purposes of giving Communion to the sick (*DS* 1654, 1657). The Council encouraged the practice of public exposition and processions, insisting that adoration of Christ in the sacrament of the Eucharist is not idolatrous (*DS* 1656).

Jesus waits for us in this sacrament of love.

Some people seem to have thought that Vatican II, with its emphasis on active participation in the liturgy and on reception of Holy Communion, implicitly discouraged practices such as eucharistic adoration and Benediction of the Blessed Sacrament. But Paul VI in 1965, before the council ended, published an encyclical on the Eucharist in which he asserted that adoration of the Blessed Sacrament had a basis in the writings of Christian antiquity and had risen to great heights in the thirteenth century, when the feast of Corpus Christi was extended to the universal Church. In the concluding section of his encyclical, he taught that the Blessed Sacrament should always be kept in a place of honor in the Church and urged the Christian faithful to make frequent visits to it.

Pope John Paul II has always had a great personal devotion to the Eucharist, both within and beyond the celebration of Mass. In his letter *Dominicae Cenae* of 1980, he affirmed the value of "various forms of eucharistic devotion: personal prayer before the Blessed Sacrament, Hours of Adoration, periods of exposition—short, prolonged, and annual (Forty Hours)—eucharistic benediction, eucharistic processions, eucharistic congresses," and the like (*DC* 3). He expressed particular esteem for the feast of Corpus Christi, instituted in the thirteenth century by his predecessor, Urban IV.

"The Church and the world," he concluded, "have a great need of eucharistic worship. Jesus waits for us in this sacrament of love. Let us be generous with our time in going to meet him in adoration and in contemplation that is full of faith and ready to make reparation for the great faults and crimes of the world. May our adoration never cease" (*DC* 3). At various eucharistic congresses, Pope John Paul has encouraged eucharistic processions and ceremonies of adoration.

> Those of you who are doubtful of the meaning of your vocation or of the value of your service: think of the places where people anxiously await a priest, and where for many years, feeling the lack of such a priest, they do not cease to hope for his presence. And sometimes it happens that they meet in an abandoned shrine, and place on the altar a stole which they still keep, and recite all the prayers of the Eucharistic Liturgy; and then, at the moment that corresponds to the transubstantiation a deep silence comes down upon them . . . so ardently do they desire to hear the words that only the lips of a priest can efficaciously utter . . . . So deeply do they feel the absence of a priest among them! . . . Such places are not lacking in the world.
> —John Paul II
> Holy Thursday
> letter 1979

Those who are pastors will know how to promote and sustain these kinds of eucharistic devotion, following the guidelines in the Roman ritual pertaining to "Holy Communion and Worship Outside Mass" and the regulations of the bishops in the United States and the local diocesan bishop. Visits to the reserved sacrament of course require no special permission. But adoration of the Blessed Sacrament exposed in a ciborium or monstrance is under the vigilance of the local ordinary, who determines what is pastorally appropriate. Perpetual adoration is permitted only when there is a religious community or a pious association of the laity who assume responsibility to see to it that all the requirements are met, including adequate care of the place and a sufficiency of worshipers at all times.

We priests should set an example of reverence for the reserved sacrament.

We priests should set an example of reverence for the reserved sacrament. In that connection the words of Pope John Paul II deserve to be recalled. At a General Audience of June 9, 1993, he said:

> To priests the Council [Vatican II] also recommends, in addition to the daily celebration of the Mass, personal devotion to the Holy Eucharist, and especially that "daily colloquy with Christ," a visit to and veneration of the Most Holy Eucharist (*PO* 18). Faith in and love for the Eucharist cannot allow Christ's presence in the tabernacle to remain alone (cf. *CCC* 1418). Already in the Old Testament we read that God dwelt in a "tent" (or "tabernacle"), which was called the "meeting tent" (Ex 33:7). The meeting was desired by God. It can be said that in the tabernacle of the Eucharist too Christ is present in view of a dialogue with his new people and with individual believers. The presbyter is the first one called to enter this meeting tent, to visit Christ in the tabernacle for a "daily talk."[9]

To bring these reflections to a close, let me add one more quotation from John Paul II. In an address of 1984 to priests he declared:

> Never believe that the yearning for intimate conversation with the eucharistic Jesus, the hours spent on your knees before the tabernacle, will halt or slow down the dynamism of your ministry. The exact opposite is true. What is given to God is never lost for man.[10]

WHAT I TRULY WANTED
Rev. Peter Murphy

———

As a boy and altar server, the Mass had always been a significant part of my life. When I became a priest, presiding at Eucharist was something special for me. However, it eventually became painful, particularly on Sundays, and I felt emotionally drained afterward. I decided to leave ministry with the intent to marry and was out of priesthood for fourteen years.

I would like to recall the priority of prayer over action since it is on prayer that the effectiveness of action depends.
—Cardinal Cláudio Hummes[11]

After I left the ministry, I still went to Mass frequently, but if I missed a Sunday or two it would not bother me. However, my devotion to the Mass was eventually renewed and I made sure that I never missed. When an old priest friend died in 2000, I knew it was time for me to return.

During my absence from ministry, my prayer life had deepened significantly. I had a practice of meditating for thirty minutes each morning and evening. With this background, after I returned to the altar, I became very aware of *praying* the Mass, particularly giving pauses for silence at appropriate times. And I have a strong sense that the people are with me in this prayer.

I can say without a doubt that these years that I have been back in active ministry have been the happiest of my life, even though, at times, the difficulties have been great. My time away gave me the advantage of seeing the essence of the priestly ministry, namely, the celebration of Eucharist, the Liturgy of the Hours, and a regular prayer practice. In fact, I feel most a priest when celebrating the Eucharist. I needed to experience being lost before finding what I truly wanted.

A Monastic Yearning for Christ
Rev. Kevin Walsh, O.C.S.O.

——

I served as a parish priest for twenty-three years before I entered a Trappist monastery eight years ago. I left the daily ordering of my life in the service of God's people to come apart and live by a different ordering of my daily life.

A monastic day is ordered in such a way that the statement, "the Eucharist is the source and summit of our lives," has acquired a richer meaning for me. Monks take the stance that the Eucharist is the heart or center of our day, our life, literally. All of our praying leads to and from it. And the monastic life has intensified my

> In the tabernacle of the Eucharist, too, Christ is present. . . . The presbyter is the first one called to enter this meeting tent, to visit Christ in the tabernacle for a "daily talk."
> —John Paul II[12]

longing for and experience of the unique meeting moment that is "God with us" in the bread that has become Jesus' body and the wine that is now Jesus' blood. The monastic yearning to encounter Christ is fulfilled again and again, never diminishing the yearning, always expanding the desire for union with God.

I make my way to the monastery church each morning at 3:00 a.m. to spend the first five-and-a-half hours of every day in a rhythm of common and private prayer. It is a constant engagement

29

with the reality of God breaking into my life, into my thoughts and my emotions. It is an awakening to the truth that we are never not "in God" and that the remembrance of God's never failing activity on our behalf both comforts and challenges me at the same time.

I find myself after each of the hours and whenever I can, making my way to pray before the Blessed Sacrament, where the silence of the day meets a silence filled with promise and presence that elicits in me a feeling of both thanksgiving and praise.

> The continuous development of the cult of eucharistic adoration is one of the most marvelous experiences of the Church. The extraordinary sanctity which has developed from it, and the number of whole communities specifically consecrated to this adoration are a guarantee of the authenticity of its inspiration. Someone like Brother Charles de Foucauld, alone in the desert with the Eucharist, yet shining out in the Church through his "Little Brothers" and "Little Sisters," is a most striking example of this in our own time.
> —Cardinal Gabriele M. Garron[13]

WHO IS CHRIST PRESENT IN THE EUCHARIST?
Rev. Msgr. John J. Strynkowski

———

It happened one Sunday morning a number of years ago. I regret that it had not happened earlier in my years as a priest, but I am glad it did not happen later.

I was at the front entrance of the church, vested and accompanied by all the ministers for the liturgy. Parishioners were still arriving and, as I watched, I realized how many of their stories I knew: the recently widowed woman struggling with loneliness, the parents with the autistic child, the wife with the alcoholic husband, and on and on. I was suddenly struck with great anxiety because I knew that this Eucharist had to be sustenance for them for the week to come, and I had to work hard to make sure that it was.

The celebration of Sunday Eucharist is an increasingly humbling and challenging experience as I come to know the parishioners better.

Ever since then, the celebration of Sunday Eucharist is an increasingly humbling and challenging experience as I come to know the parishioners better and better. As they gather for the Eucharist with their joys and sorrows, I realize the significance of this moment for their lives and I want to respond to it by presiding and preaching in a way that will make this sacrificial meal true nourishment for their lives. Theologically I know that the Eucharist is effective *ex opere operato*, but there is much I can do to make it more fruitful.

31

I am often awed by the faith, courage, perseverance, and love in the face of difficult circumstances that many parishioners demonstrate. They are frequently dealing with immense sorrows within their families. As a priest friend of mine said, "Behind every family there is a mess." And so they come to the Sunday Eucharist for strength. It is true that the Lord himself is present, offering that strength, but I must work with him or, at the very least, not stand in his way.

Who, then, is the Lord Jesus Christ present in the Eucharist, and how do I work with him in the celebration of the liturgy? That question is as inexhaustible as the very mystery of Jesus Christ himself. Obviously he is present as Son of God and Son of Man, the crucified and risen Lord, judge of the living and the dead, wisdom that maintains the order of the universe, font of mercy, reconciler and peacemaker, and so on in a vast litany of images from scripture through centuries of tradition. But there are three aspects of his presence, based on his earthly ministry, that have been particularly important for me and guide me in my preaching and celebration. Jesus Christ is present as *compassionate shepherd, living bread,* and *giver of hope.*

Jesus Christ is present as compassionate shepherd, living bread, and giver of hope.

Compassionate Shepherd

In the second half of the 1990s I was pastor of a Polish parish. Most of the parishioners were recent immigrants. One summer an eight-year-old Polish girl was killed in a tragic railroad accident. The day after the funeral in our church, I celebrated the 8:00 a.m. Polish Mass. Everyone was in their usual seat, but there was someone in the back of the church whom I could not recognize in the dim light. At Communion time, I was profoundly moved when I saw it was the mother of the little girl. I admired the incredible faith that led her to the Eucharist the day after her daughter's funeral. Did she, in some unspoken way, know Jesus to be the compassionate shepherd?

On several occasions during his public ministry Jesus fed the crowds who were following him. We recognize these meals as anticipations of the Last Supper and ultimately the Eucharist itself. One of these meals is particularly significant because of what it tells us about who Jesus is in the Eucharist. In the Gospel according to St. Matthew we read that after John the Baptist had been beheaded and his disciples had buried his body, "they went and told Jesus." And then, Matthew continues, "When Jesus heard of it, he withdrew in a boat from there to a deserted place by himself" (Mt 14:12–13).

We can hardly imagine the grief that Jesus must have felt at the news of John the Baptist's martyrdom. He had lost not only a life-long companion, not only a powerful and dynamic preacher, but also the one appointed by God to prepare the way for him. Jesus must also have grieved because he was experiencing the deep-rooted cruelty manifested by Herod, Herodias, and her daughter. And he probably also could now foresee more clearly the destiny that awaited him. In grief, then, Jesus withdrew "to a deserted place by himself."

His heart was filled with pity for them, for they were like sheep without a shepherd.

Jesus, however, did not have much time to grieve. "The crowds . . . followed him on foot from their towns" (v 13). He could not ignore their presence and their yearning for his healing words and actions. "When he disembarked and saw the vast crowd, his heart was moved with pity for them, and he cured their sick" (v 14). In the Gospel according to St. Mark this reaction of pity from Jesus for the crowd has an added and extremely important detail: "When he disembarked and saw the vast crowd, his heart was filled with pity for them, for they were like sheep without a shepherd; and he began to teach them many things" (Mk 6:34).

When I reflect on these words, it seems to me that one of the sources of Jesus' compassion for the crowd was his own grief at the death of John the Baptist. His own feeling of loss enabled him to enter into the feelings of loss and grief that his followers were experiencing or would experience in their lives. The hunger of the crowd for his presence did not allow him to grieve alone. He responded to them with the care of a shepherd for his sheep and with the compassion of one who knows his grief and the grief of his followers.

Jesus is the compassionate shepherd. This is obvious when Matthew tells us that he cures the sick. But we should note also Mark's words that Jesus "began to teach them many things." This imparting of wisdom and knowledge of the Father is compassionate shepherding. "He ordered the crowds to sit down on the grass. Taking the five loaves and the two fish, and looking up to heaven, he said the blessing, broke the loaves, and gave them to the disciples, who in turn gave them to the crowd. They all ate and were satisfied" (Mt 14:19–20). Here is the Eucharist in its most original form: teaching and feeding, the structure that later became the Liturgy of the Word and the Liturgy of the Eucharist.

It is my hope that I celebrate the Eucharist in a way that reveals the compassion of Christ.

All of this is for "curing the sick." They are not necessarily only the physically ill. They can also be those who are spiritually hurt. In the Eucharist they encounter Christ the compassionate shepherd who teaches, feeds, and heals. Is this why, through the centuries, Christians have come to the Eucharist, or to use the words of the Jesuit poet Gerard Manley Hopkins, have come to the "hero of Calvary, Christ's feet"? It is the sublime privilege of the priest to be the transparent witness to the compassionate shepherd in the Eucharist.

It is my hope that I celebrate the Eucharist in a way that reveals the compassion of Christ. The special moment when I can exhibit that compassion is the homily. Pope Benedict XVI has frequently said that too often people think of Christianity as a religion of prohibitions. He reminds us that it is anything but that. The homily is not a harangue. It gives us the opportunity to show forth in a positive way the "poetry" of God's revelation as we encounter it in the scripture readings and the liturgical season. It also gives us the opportunity to proclaim God's compassion exhibited in his endless mercy.

There is a striking passage in Pope Benedict XVI's encyclical *Deus Caritas Est* that ought to drive our homilies: "God's passionate love for his people—for humanity—is at the same time a forgiving love. It is so great that it turns God against himself, his love against his justice" (10). In Jesus, the compassionate shepherd, that overwhelming love, is startlingly concrete.

BREAD OF LIFE

When I met a certain Polish cardinal in Brooklyn in the autumn of 1969, I could not have anticipated that nine years later he would be elected Bishop of Rome, Pope John Paul II. I came to know him somewhat in the intervening years and subsequently had the blessing of concelebrating the Eucharist with him in his private chapel. Many have had that experience and all will attest how intensely prayerful it was. My memory of that experience continues to nourish me even years later.

Jesus sums up this arc of his life in the simple phenomenon of bread that is broken and eaten.

The sixth chapter of the Gospel according to St. John contains Jesus' discourse on himself as the bread of life come down from heaven. Perhaps the crucial sentence of this discourse is found in verse 51: "The bread that I will give is my flesh for the life of the world." In these few words, Jesus describes the entire arc of his life from incarnation to crucifixion. The flesh that the word assumed at the beginning is surrendered on the cross for the life of the world. Jesus sums up this arc of his life in the simple phenomenon of bread that is broken and eaten.

Why bread? I want to suggest that there is a remarkable symmetry between bread and the life, death, and resurrection of Jesus, and ultimately ourselves as well. I begin with bread itself. Bread is ordinary stuff, everyday food that we easily take for granted. At the same time it has substance, especially the dark, dense breads that are to be found in some European countries. Because bread has substance, it is nourishing. But for bread to be nourishing it has to be broken and eaten.

We do not know what Jesus looked like. It is probably not farfetched to say that he looked like an ordinary person of his time and culture. Certainly his life in Nazareth was that of an ordinary Israelite. But his emergence into public ministry revealed the extraordinary substance of a presence revealing the Father, showing itself in the wisdom of speech and the power of miraculous deeds. Because of that substance, people found nourishment for their lives in his words and actions. They discovered meaning, hope, and love. But for Jesus to be nourishment he had to undergo the brokenness of betrayal, torture, and crucifixion. This brought the substance of the work he received from the Father to its completion "for the life of the world."

We priests are basically ordinary folk. We are by no means among the great of this world. On the contrary, we are often looked down upon. But because of our spiritual and academic formation in the incredibly rich tradition of the Church, because of our prayer and union with the Lord, because we are so often unsparing of ourselves in our ministries, we offer substance to people's lives. It is a substance that nourishes them because it gives them meaning and communion with the Lord and the entire Christian community. But we cannot nourish others without self-sacrifice, without the discipline of spiritual life, without the expenditure of energy, without anxiety for those who are lost, without the risk of being misunderstood or, at times, judged unfairly.

We cannot nourish others without self-sacrifice.

Bread, Jesus, priests—ordinary, substantial, nourishing, broken. For what purpose? So that Christians too, mostly ordinary, can themselves be substantial in the ways of the Lord and nourishing for all whom they meet. So that they can understand that no great good is achieved without the brokenness of the cross.

All this comes together in the remarkable sacrifice of the Eucharist—bread, Jesus Christ, the priest, the community. "Because the loaf of bread is one, we, though many, are one body, for we all partake of the one loaf" (1 Cor 10:17). As priests, we bring the ecclesial body of Christ together to be nourished by his eucharistic body. This is the summit of the Church's prayer, requiring us to be men of prayer not only during the Eucharist but always. We cannot truly pray at the Eucharist if prayer is not the constant substance and nourishment of our lives. We cannot truly pray at the Eucharist if we do not bring to prayer our own brokenness and the brokenness of priesthood today, as well as the brokenness of the Church and the world.

GIVER OF HOPE

Funeral homilies are probably the most challenging for us. We want to offer people hope. As a source of hope, I sometimes use the image of our lives as composed of many threads that are not yet woven into a full tapestry. There is much that is puzzling about each one of us—even to ourselves—and it is the Lord in the Kingdom who resolves all the puzzles, weaving the threads of our lives into a complete and beautiful tapestry that none of us could create. Only one person in the course of human history did that—Jesus, on the night before he died. In a masterful way he interwove the traditions of his people, the deeds of his life, and the yearnings of all human beings.

Jesus fulfills God's promise to renew his saving deeds in the midst of all who gather to remember.

Jesus held the Last Supper in the context of Israel's celebration of Passover, the most important feast of the Jewish calendar. Those who celebrated saw themselves as included among that first generation that God led from slavery in Egypt toward the Promised Land. In the instructions for the celebration of Passover, Moses tells future generations: "On this day you shall explain to your son, 'This is because of what the Lord did for me when I came out of Egypt'" (Ex 13:8). God's saving deed in the past is made present as succeeding generations celebrate Passover. God promises to renew the powerful grace of the Exodus for those who gather to remember in the future.

At the Last Supper, Jesus commands his disciples to remember what he did. He thus makes it possible for his saving deeds to be present for all generations as his followers gather for the Eucharist. Jesus' death and resurrection and our participation in it is the new Exodus and the new Passover: "Christ our Passover has been sacrificed" (1 Cor 5:7). Jesus fulfills God's promise to renew his saving deeds in the midst of all who gather to remember.

Essential to the eucharistic spirituality of the priest is the joy of his celebration.

Through the prophet Isaiah, God promised to send a servant of whom he says: "I formed you, and set you as a covenant of the people, a light for the nations" (Is 42:6). Similarly through the prophet Jeremiah, God says that he "will make a new covenant with the house of Israel and the house of Judah" (Jer 31:31). Essential to this covenant, God says, is that "All, from least to greatest, shall know me . . . for I will forgive their evildoing and remember their sin no more" (Jer 31:34).

At the Last Supper, Jesus declares: "This cup is the new covenant in my blood" (1 Cor 11:25). In the Gospel according to St. Matthew, Jesus says that his blood, "the blood of the covenant," is "to be shed on behalf of many for the forgiveness of sins" (Mt 26:28). And in the Gospel according to St. Luke, Jesus at the Last Supper reminds his disciples, "I am in your midst as the one who serves you" (Lk 22:27). The promises of God through the prophets for a new covenant for the forgiveness of sins established by the servant whom God sends are fulfilled by Jesus at the Last Supper, on the cross, and perpetually through the Eucharist.

At the Last Supper, Jesus makes a promise: "From now on I shall not drink this fruit of the vine until the day when I drink it with you new in the kingdom of my Father" (Mt 26:29). In this way, Jesus tells us that he will gather all of us who are united in the Eucharist at the great heavenly feast. We can believe his promise because he himself was faithful to all the promises of God. Thus he gives hope to us as we come to the Eucharist, especially those of us who walk with him now on a painful *via crucis*.

Through the simple gestures and brief words of the Last Supper, Jesus wove together the promises and traditions of the past, the work of God in and through him, and the hope of the coming kingdom. Essential to the eucharistic spirituality of the priest is the joy of his celebration as he recalls the saving sacrifice of Christ, acknowledges the grace at work in the assembly, and looks to the consummation of the Eucharist in the heavenly feast. That joy should translate into hopeful words and demeanor that encourage, ennoble, and enthuse a pilgrim people.

The Sunday Eucharist can be the one moment of the week where everyone can sense a welcome, harmony, and unity that is not otherwise available.

The heavenly feast will be a gathering of all nations. Even now so many of our Sunday celebrations are gatherings of people from many nations. In everyday life there are tensions and conflicts that arise from the pluralistic nature of our society. The Sunday Eucharist can be the one moment of the week where, through the sacrament itself and our leadership, everyone can sense a welcome, harmony, and unity that is not otherwise available. The eucharistic community is an anticipation of the heavenly feast that confirms our hope in the Lord's plan to bring to completion the mystery of our lives and the history of humanity. As priests, we are signs of that hope by our work for reconciliation within individuals and communities leading to and flowing from the communion of the Eucharist. We are weavers apprenticed to the master weaver.

A number of years ago for about a month I brought Holy Communion to a young man dying of AIDS. He was twenty-four years old and, since it was late September, I told him about St. Therese of Lisieux. When he heard that she was twenty-four at her death, his eyes lit up and he wanted me to tell him more about her. Shortly after, the doctors told him that there was nothing more that medicine could do for him. When I came back the next day, the walls of his room, which had been covered with "Get Well" messages, were bare, except for the image of St. Therese opposite his bed. He must have spent hours looking at that image. He died several days later. I believe that I had been a messenger of hope for him. Bringing him Holy Communion, I also linked him to the communion of saints. He now had another thread for his life and for the tapestry the Lord had woven for him in eternity.

CONCLUSION

In the apse of the Basilica of St. Paul Outside the Walls in Rome, there is a mosaic of Christ the ruler of all in majesty. The figure of Christ dominates the apse and the sanctuary. At his feet there is the tiny figure of Pope Honorius III who, around AD 1220, had ordered that this mosaic be installed. The Pope is prostrate in awe and humility before Christ. I suggest that he represents all priests in their celebration of the Eucharist.

It is with awe and humility that we are called to serve not only the Lord in the inexhaustible mystery of who he is, but also all who come to him seeking the compassionate shepherd, the bread of life, the giver of hope. Some come with great anguish. We celebrate the Eucharist with them, not as holding some special worldly power, but as their humble servants in imitation of him who at the Last Supper first washed the feet of his disciples.

On that Sunday long ago, I felt great anxiety as I recognized the suffering and wounds of so many coming to the Eucharist. I have been a priest since 1963 and I still feel some anxiety as I prepare for the liturgy. But

> Some years ago a national body of liturgical leaders surveyed Catholics to determine their criteria for evaluating a weekend Eucharistic liturgy. Preaching headed the list. The average person, according to that study, judges the quality of a Mass by the quality of the homily.
> —Joseph M. Champlin[14]

I feel humility even more because the members of Christ's body, the Church, come seeking compassion, nourishment, and hope. I am the Lord's instrument for that purpose. And they too show me compassion, nourish me, and give me hope by their faith and presence. All of this is the overwhelmingly great mystery and work of the Lord Jesus Christ in the Eucharist.

A HUNGER FOR THE EUCHARIST
Rev. Msgr. Stephen J. Rossetti

My appreciation and desire for the Eucharist has grown through my years of priesthood. This might be surprising to some who expect a priest to begin with a fully developed eucharistic spirituality. But a priest's spiritual life necessarily deepens as the years pass, and I have found my appreciation and longing for the Eucharist to have steadily intensified.

This personal experience has revealed to me the truth of the Church's teaching that the Eucharist is the "source and summit of the Christian life." Each day I find myself longing for the Eucharist. There is something missing until I celebrate the Mass.

Occasionally, there have been days when I have been traveling long distances, and I found myself having missed saying Mass. As the years pass, I feel an increasing emptiness and a hunger inside when this happens. For me, the Eucharist is real food and real drink, as Jesus told us. I am spiritually "famished" without it.

Recently, I read a biography of Blessed Charles de Foucauld. For a period of time when he was a hermit in the desert, he was not allowed to celebrate Mass or reserve the Blessed Sacrament, since he was alone. This was an extraordinarily difficult trial for him. Now I can understand from my own experience how great a trial that must have been.

My life as a priest centers around the Eucharist. One of the great blessings of the priesthood is our closeness to the Eucharist.

There I am close to Jesus. It is there that I am most alive. The Eucharist has truly become the center of my life.

> Let us be faithful, dear confreres, to the daily celebration of the Most Holy Eucharist, not solely in order to fulfill a pastoral commitment or a requirement of the community entrusted to us but because of the absolute personal need we have of it, as of breathing, as of light for our life, as the one satisfactory reason for a complete priestly existence.
> —Cardinal Cláudio Hummes[15]

UNIVERSAL COMMUNION
Cardinal Francis George, O.M.I.

———

A t the April 17, 2008, Mass with the Pope at Nationals Stadium in Washington, D.C., as I was praying in thanksgiving during the silence after the distribution of Holy Communion, I looked into the stadium from the sanctuary and had a profound experience of the unity in Christ that is the essence of the Church's life. The Pope is the visible center of universal communion, but Jesus, risen from the dead in the body that we had just received sacramentally, works invisibly to unite, ever more closely, all those who come to know him in his body, the Church. We know this, but sometimes we feel it; and such an experience was given me during this moment of Pope Benedict's visit to our country. After all the preparations, the security concerns, the programming to the minute, the care that all would go as planned, the Lord acts as he will to remind us who we are and to draw us into the center of our lives: life with him.

Christ has often used the Holy Eucharist in this way to guide my life and keep me centered. My sense of calling to the ordained priesthood came for the first time during my thanksgiving after receiving the Lord in my first Holy Communion. When I need to really check to see if a particular idea or plan of action is acceptable to the Lord, thanksgiving after receiving Communion is the time to make the test.

The Eucharist is the sacrament of unity, and unity is a mark of the Church. Unity is first of all a gift from Christ, prayed for at the Last Supper, bestowed at Pentecost with the gift of the Holy Spirit,

45

guaranteed through visible communion with the successor of Peter. Often, perhaps, we don't think about the fullest extent of this unity as willed by Christ himself. It is the will of Christ that all those he died to save should be gathered visibly into his body, the Church, and there receive sacramentally his eucharistic body in Holy Communion.

> We cannot approach the eucharistic table without being drawn into the mission which, beginning in the very heart of God, is meant to reach all people.
> —*Sacramentum Caritatis* 84

It is the Church's mission in this world to extend this unity. How can we receive the body of the Lord in the Eucharist and not be driven to invite all to come to know him intimately in sharing his gifts? What a great tragedy, for them and for us, that many of those baptized in other faith communities have never received the Lord sacramentally in Holy Communion.

But the universe of communion extends beyond this world. The seeds of immortality are planted in our still mortal bodies when we take and receive the risen body of the Lord in the Eucharist. The thirst for a unity, accomplished only in the heavenly banquet, deepens each time we receive Communion. This world's attractions grow paler in the light of the promised eschaton. Each place the Eucharist is celebrated becomes the center of the cosmos; each time the Mass is said this world changes. In receiving Holy Communion, the bonds of union in Christ are drawn tighter; the desire to unite people to him grows in its expanse; the gratitude for the gifts that are ours in Christ impels us to share them universally.

Eucharist as the Source of Priestly Identity
Archbishop Donald W. Wuerl

For the more than twenty years that I have been a diocesan bishop, I have tried, whenever possible, to install every pastor I appoint to a parish. The installation takes place in the context of a Saturday vigil or Sunday morning Mass, and provides me with an opportunity to remind myself and those present that the most significant action of the pastor—of every priest—is the celebration of the Eucharist. The rite for the installation of a pastor suggests that the bishop reflect with the whole parish family on the promises of the priest at his ordination, the extraordinary relationship he has with Christ, the great high priest, and the eucharistic liturgy in which the work of Christ is made present and the mystery of our redemption is carried out.

The heart of our priestly identity and the central action of our priestly ministry is the Eucharist.

In reflecting on the heart of our priestly identity and the central action of our priestly ministry—the Eucharist—I want to consider with you the uniqueness of the calling by which each priest participates in the living memorial of the death and resurrection of Christ that renews and establishes the Church over and over, identifies both the faithful and ourselves, and is the culmination on this side of heaven of our striving to be one with the Lord Jesus.

The special nature of what we are called to be and do is intimately tied to what the Church is and why Christ chose to remain with us and touch us in this manner. The Church shares in the very life of the risen Lord. Her members, through Baptism into the Church, form a body with Christ as its head. It is through the Church that women and men are saved by coming to know Jesus Christ and being united in grace to the Father through the outpouring of the Holy Spirit. This mystery of the faith necessarily involves the mystery of the Eucharist and the Church.

For all of the members of the Church spread throughout the world the principal act of worship and spiritual nourishment is the celebration of the Eucharist. Sunday Mass becomes not only an expression of our membership in the body of Christ but also our participation in the very mystery of our redemption. Since the priesthood is essential to the celebration of *Eucharist, Church,* the Eucharist, all three, Eucharist, Church, *and priesthood are* and priesthood, are intimately united. Pope *intimately united.* Benedict XVI, in his post-synodal apostolic exhortation *Sacramentum Caritatis,* puts it this way: "First of all, we need to stress once again that the connection between *Holy Orders and the Eucharist* is seen most clearly at Mass, when the bishop or priest presides *in the person of Christ the Head*" (*S Car* 23).

Many years ago, I had the occasion to visit the Church of the Assumption in the tiny island of Torcello, in the same lagoon that is home to its larger and better known relatives, Venice, Morano, and Burano. What struck me about this ancient ninth-century church building that once served as the cathedral of Torcello was, first of all, that it gave testimony to just how ancient is this devotion to Mary under the title of her Assumption into heaven, and secondly that the sanctuary—in stone—was arranged in the clear expectation that the bishop and his priests would come together for the celebration of Mass with the rest of the faithful. The unity of the Church, with her bishop and priests around the Eucharist, was literally carved in stone.

A more recent experience of the same unity of the Church centered in the Eucharist was the Mass celebrated on April 17, 2008, at Nationals Park in Washington by our Holy Father, Pope Benedict XVI, during his apostolic journey to the United States. As we prepared for that eucharistic liturgy, we hoped to have the Pope experience the face and voice of the Church in our nation. The richness of the ethnic and cultural diversity of the Catholic Church was clearly visible. As the music at Mass demonstrated, the Church is vibrant, always young and expressive of the faith.

In the midst of the great variety of backgrounds, what came through was a oneness in faith and devotion. Many were struck by the reverent silence that pervaded the crowd of nearly fifty thousand people during the Eucharistic Prayer. I recall that the only real noise at that point came from outside the park. It was a testimony to the power of the Eucharist to make us all one—one in faith, hope, love, and new life in Christ. After the Mass, it was not a surprise that the Pope remarked: "That liturgy was a true prayer."

SALVATION FROM CHRIST IN THE CHURCH

The work of redemption did not end when Christ returned in glory to his Father but continues today and until the last day. "Behold I am with you always, until the end of the age" (Mt 28:20). Jesus' presence in the Church that he established continues so that his work of bridging the gap between God and mankind might go on. Thus the Church takes on the characteristics of its divine founder and Lord. The Church is his body. Christ is the head, and we are the members. Membership in the Church is, then, membership in Christ, drawing life and truth from him. As members of the Church, his body, we come to know Christ, to become one with him and to attain our salvation through him. Only in and through the Church can we find that continuity with the experience and teaching of the apostles that verifies and authenticates our own personal faith. In and through the Church we come

Membership in the Church is membership in Christ, drawing life and truth from him.

to encounter the living Lord not just as an historical reality, but also as a living person present to us sacramentally as brother and savior.

Just as salvation and grace come to us through Jesus, so do they continue to reach us through his Church. That is why Christ founded his Church. We are not just related individually and directly to God but also as God's family united with Christ. It is in and through Christ present and manifest in his Church that we come to God. The mediatorship of Christ continues in the visible, sacramental Church that we identify as the one, holy, catholic, and apostolic communion of saints.

To be a priest is to see our very being as part of the mystery of Christ continuing to be with his people.

In this we differ from those who accept personal faith alone as the means of salvation. To be a Catholic is to recognize the role of the Church, not as incidental or secondary to salvation, but as the very means created and given to us by Jesus so that his work, accomplished in his death and resurrection, might be re-presented in our day and applied to us. To be a priest is to see our very being as part of the mystery of Christ continuing to be with his people. We, in the sacramental life of the Church, realize the very presence and life-giving touch of Jesus for those we serve.

A DISTINCT DIOCESAN SPIRITUALITY

Often, we hear the question: is there a distinct spirituality of the diocesan priesthood? This question arises in part from the experience of many priests of an identifiable spirituality reflected in religious communities of men—often evident within the seminary and its formation program. Easily recognizable are forms of spirituality noted as Franciscan, Benedictine, Sulpician, or other. Is there a spirituality unique to the diocesan priest?

The answer is found in our grasp of the ministry of the priest, which is so intimately tied to sacraments and particularly the celebration of the Eucharist. Here, in these sacred moments, which the Church speaks of as privileged encounters with Christ, not only does the priest make present Christ's redemptive action, but he also participates in the mystery of Christ's enduring presence in his Church. As Christ is personally at work in the sacraments, he is there both for the one who receives the sacrament and for the priest who administers it. Hence we, as priests, are almost continually in an encounter with the Lord that transcends the limits of our day and places us in the realm of grace, in the depths of the kingdom coming to be. *This is both our ministry and our identity.*

It was to remind us of our connection with the Lord—through the Church and her apostolic ministry—that our Holy Father, Pope Benedict XVI, pointed out this reality in his homily at Nationals Park. "In the exercise of my ministry as the Successor of Peter, I have come to America to confirm you, my brothers and sisters, in the faith of the apostles" (cf. Lk 22:32).

We as priests are living links in a chain reaching back over twenty centuries to contact the very person of Christ.

We as priests are living links in a chain reaching back over twenty centuries to contact the very person of Christ and reaching forward through and beyond time and the human condition to Christ, his kingdom and the fullness of his glory. We—as ministers of the mysteries of salvation—are guardians of the memory, the memorial of the death and resurrection of Christ. This memory, because it effects what it memorializes, gives the distinct quality to the actions that identify us and provides the frame of reference for our priestly spirituality.

On occasion I have to be in Rome. Recently I was there for the Synod of Bishops on the Word of God. The North American College always provides a place to stay and, in a longstanding tradition, I try always to have Mass with our priests and seminarians who are studying in the Eternal City. We go early in the morning to Saint Peter's Basilica so that we can get an altar as close as possible to the tomb of Saint Peter. That liturgy says so much. We are part of a living tradition that connects us to Peter and the apostles, which in turn authenticates our own ministry. When we hear, "Do this in memory of me," in these circumstances, we cannot help but feel the impact of the Church's doctrine on apostolic tradition and apostolic succession. From the beginning—because of her priesthood—the Church did and continues to do what the Servant of God Pope John Paul II so beautifully describes in *Ecclesia de Eucharistia*:

> The Apostles, by accepting in the Upper Room Jesus' invitation: "Take, eat", "Drink of it, all of you" (Mt 26:26–27), entered for the first time into sacramental communion with him. From that time forward, until the end of the age, the Church is built up through sacramental communion with the Son of God who was sacrificed for our sake: "Do this in remembrance of me. . . . do this, as often as you drink it, in remembrance of me" (1 Cor 11:24–25; cf Lk 22:19). (*EE* 21)

Jesus' New Memorial

The night before he was to undergo his passion and death, Jesus established a new memorial—a new way to recall and to remember what he was about to endure. The three synoptic gospels and Saint Paul have handed on to us the account of the institution of the Eucharist. Saint John for his part reports the words of Jesus in the synagogue of Capernaum that prepare for the institution of the Eucharist: Christ calls himself the bread of life, come down from heaven (Jn 6).

We are part of a living tradition that connects us to Peter and the apostles.

Paul beautifully describes the Last Supper in his first letter to the Corinthians:

> For I have received from the Lord what I also handed on to you, that the Lord Jesus, on the night he was handed over, took bread, and, after he had given thanks, broke it and said, "This is my body that is for you. Do this in remembrance of me." In the same way also the cup, after supper, saying, "This cup is the new covenant in my blood. Do this, as often as you drink it, in remembrance

of me." For as often as you eat this bread and drink the cup, you proclaim the death of the Lord until he comes. (1 Cor 11:24–26)

This ongoing proclamation and making present of the Lord happens in a ritualized setting that looks back to God's previous intervention among men to form, explain, and understand it. The context of the new memorial—instituted at the Last Supper—is the Jewish Passover, the ritual meal established at God's command to help the Jewish people remember the events of their deliverance from Egypt and the gracious loving-kindness of God, who is their deliverer. This recalling, remembering, would be more than nostalgia. It would somehow keep present and actual the effect of past saving events.

Priests fulfill their chief duty in the mystery of the Eucharistic Sacrifice.
—Presbyterorum Ordinis *13*

In an age before technology, where there were no cameras, photographs, or camcorders, the ways in which events were remembered and passed on were through the celebrations and ritualized reminders that formed the history, frame of reference, and calendar for a people, in this case, God's people. This was the way people recalled what happened to them in the past, its significance for them in the present, and why it is important to continue the memory in the future.

In the book of Exodus we read how at God's instructions, Moses fashioned a memorial meal—a ritual presentation of the Passover events. The meal was thus integrally connected with the circumstances of the liberation. The symbols of nourishment taken in community and eaten in haste while preparing for flight captured in ritual what God was about to effect in history.

Added to this was the Lord's special command to repeat these ceremonies in the future:

This day shall be a memorial feast for you, which all your generations shall celebrate with pilgrimage to the Lord, as a perpetual institution. . . . Since it was on this very day that I brought your ranks out of the land of Egypt,

you must celebrate this day throughout your generations
as a perpetual institution. (Ex 12:14, 17)

MEMORIAL MAKES PAST EVENTS PRESENT

This whole series of saving events was richly preserved in the
annual repetition of the Passover meal in a
"memorial feast." As generation after generation shared the paschal lamb and the unleav-
ened bread, fathers told their children of the
wonders God had worked on behalf of his
chosen people. In this memorial feast they
understood and celebrated far more than a
community festival. The Passover meal was
not simply an opportunity to review past his-
tory. In this meal the people of God knew they were with their
Lord, and they renewed the covenant he had made with them.

*The interplay
between ritual and
history that took
place in the Exodus
was repeated at
the new Pasch.*

As the *Catechism of the Catholic Church* teaches us:

> In the sense of Sacred Scripture the *memorial* is not
> merely the recollection of past events but the proclama-
> tion of the mighty works wrought by God for men. In
> the liturgical celebration of these events, they become in
> a certain way present and real. This is how Israel under-
> stands its liberation from Egypt: every time Passover is
> celebrated, the Exodus events are made present to the
> memory of believers so that they may conform their lives
> to them. (*CCC* 1363)

The interplay between ritual and history that took place in
the Exodus was repeated at the new Pasch. Christ's death, which is
the sacrificial offering that frees us from sin, and his resurrection,
which brings us to new life, took place after the Last Supper, just
as the flight from Egypt and the events of Sinai followed the first
Passover meal. But Jesus' command to repeat this as a "memorial"
of himself established the Last Supper as the ceremonial setting for
the re-presentation of the events of our salvation. In this memorial

sacrifice the new covenant could and would be constantly renewed with every succeeding generation.

Like the Passover meal that was the context of the Last Supper and that was intended to remind the Jewish people of their formation as God's people and therefore their identity, the Eucharist was intended to be a memorial. But it was much more. It was a sacramental remembering that would actually make the event it memorialized present, not as a memory but as a reality. In the New Testament, the memorial takes on new meaning. When the Church celebrates the Eucharist, it commemorates Christ's Passover and it is made present: the sacrifice Christ offered once for all on the cross remains ever-present.

> *The priest is the personal, indispensable link bringing Christ sacramentally but really to the lives of those who come to the memorial meal.*

When we focus on the Eucharist we recognize its immediate connectedness to the Last Supper. The origins of the Eucharist are found in the Last Supper. The *Catechism* teaches us:

> In order to leave them a pledge of this love, in order never to depart from his own and to make them sharers in his Passover, he instituted the Eucharist as a memorial of his death and resurrection, and commanded his apostles to celebrate it until his return; "thereby he constituted them priests of the New Testament." (*CCC* 1337)

NOT BYSTANDERS, BUT PARTICIPANTS

The Eucharist is intended to lift up for us once again the events of our salvation, but to do so in a way that we actually participate in those saving actions. The Church calls us not just to a commemoration of the events of two thousand years ago, as laudable as that might be, but also to enter the mystery itself today. We are not bystanders, but rather participants. Essential to this interaction of heaven and earth is the priest. He is the personal, indispensable link bringing Christ sacramentally but really to the lives of those who come to the memorial meal, to the Holy Sacrifice of the Mass.

In his encyclical on the Eucharist that I have already quoted, Pope John Paul II reminds us of the ancient faith of the Church:

When we speak of a priest's spirituality, we necessarily focus on the Eucharist.

"When the Church celebrates the Eucharist, the memorial of her Lord's death and resurrection, this central event of salvation becomes really present and 'the work of our redemption is carried out'" (*EE* 11).

As the Second Vatican Council's Constitution on the Sacred Liturgy teaches:

> At the Last Supper, on the night He was betrayed, our Savior instituted the eucharistic sacrifice of his body and blood. He did this in order to perpetuate the sacrifice of the cross throughout the centuries until He should come again, and so to entrust to his beloved spouse, the Church, a memorial of his death and resurrection: a sacrament of love, a sign of unity, a bond of charity, a paschal banquet in which Christ is received, the mind is filled with grace, and a pledge of future life is given to us. (*SC* 47)

Unlike any other form of remembrance or commemoration, the Mass—the eucharistic liturgy—thanks to God's gracious gift, the outpouring of the Holy Spirit, has the power to make present the very reality it symbolizes.

A PRIEST'S ONENESS WITH CHRIST

When we speak of a priest's spirituality, we necessarily focus on the Eucharist. It is here that our oneness with Christ, as we are configured to Christ as head, becomes intelligible in a new and demanding way. In the eucharistic liturgy, we find not only the principal pastoral action that gives identity to our lives but the strength—the spiritual power—to live out that reality in all of its vigor. It is in this mystery of our salvation that we, like those whom we serve, actually encounter Christ. But for priests, we meet him at the level of identity—of oneness. Our spiritual life is rooted and nurtured by this constant realized memorial in which we, as Christ, act and are united. As in the prayer of Saint Richard of Chichester, may we come each and every day to "know you (Christ) more clearly, love you more dearly and follow you more nearly. . . ."

There is nothing I do or can do that can come anywhere near to the grace and life-giving action I am blessed to realize in the celebration of Mass.

Pope Benedict XVI in *Sacramentum Caritatis* taught us about the connection of each of the sacraments with the Eucharist. Our mystery—our identity as priests, our ongoing encounter with the Lord Jesus—finds its principal resonance in the Eucharist and the sacraments that are "bound up with the Eucharist." As our Holy Father reminds us:

> The Second Vatican Council recalled that "all the sacraments, and indeed all ecclesiastical ministries and works of the apostolate, are bound up with the Eucharist and are directed towards it. For in the most blessed Eucharist is contained the entire spiritual wealth of the Church, namely Christ himself our Pasch and our living bread, who gives life to humanity through his flesh—that flesh which is given life and gives life by the Holy Spirit. Thus men and women are invited and led to offer themselves, their works and all creation in union with Christ" (*Presbyterorum Ordinis* 5). This close relationship of the Eucharist with the other sacraments and the Christian life can be most fully understood when we contemplate the mystery of the Church herself as a sacrament. (*S Car* 16)

Thus every time we as priests exercise our ministry at the baptismal font through the outpouring of water and the Holy Spirit, or in the sacrament of Reconciliation when sins are absolved, or in the Anointing of the Sick when Christ's physical and spiritual healing power is present, or when we preside at a marriage where the power of God is at work, and certainly in the sacrament of the Eucharist where we consecrate the bread and wine, making them the body and blood of Christ, do we truly find the source of our own spirituality and the nurture of the life of the Spirit within us.

I have always tried to appreciate that there is nothing I do or can do, no matter how much time, energy, and effort I apply to it, that can come anywhere near to the grace and life-giving action I am blessed to realize in the celebration of Mass. This is true of every Mass, whether quiet and reflective with a small congregation, a large and vibrant Sunday celebration, or even a major diocesan or national eucharistic gathering. What I am doing—I remind myself—is not only what Christ asks me to do in memory of him, but to do it in his person.

BASKING IN THE EUCHARISTIC PRESENCE

Time spent before the Blessed Sacrament is an opportunity simply to bask in the light of the truth that Christ, whose servants and "images" we are, wants to fill us with his love. In quiet time preparing for the celebration of Mass, we open ourselves to be renewed in the Spirit of God who configures us to Christ as head of his Church. We are reminded in *Sacramentum Caritatis*: "In the Eucharist, the Son of God comes to meet us and desires to become one with us; eucharistic adoration is simply the natural consequence of the eucharistic celebration, which is itself the Church's supreme act of adoration" (*S Car* 66).

> It is in the Eucharistic cult or in the Eucharistic assembly of the faithful that they [priests] exercise in a supreme degree their sacred office; there, acting in the person of Christ and proclaiming his mystery, they unite the votive offerings of the faithful to the sacrifice of Christ their head. . . . From this unique sacrifice their whole priestly ministry draws its strength.
> —CCC 1566

The faith of the Church in the real presence of Jesus in the Eucharist is found in the words of Jesus himself, as recorded in the Gospel of Saint John. In the eucharistic discourse after the multiplication of the loaves, our Lord contrasted ordinary bread with a bread that is not of this world but contains eternal life for those who eat it. He said: "I am the bread of life. . . . I am the living bread that came down from heaven; whoever eats of this bread will live forever; and the bread that I will give is my flesh for the life of the world" (Jn 6:48, 51).

Faith that Jesus is truly present in the sacrament led believers to worship Christ dwelling with us permanently in the sacrament. Wherever the sacrament is, there is Christ who is our Lord and our God. Hence he is ever to be worshiped in this mystery. Such worship is expressed in many ways: in genuflection before the tabernacle, in adoration of the Eucharist, and in the many forms of eucharistic devotion that faith has nourished.

CALLED TO MAKE CHRIST PRESENT

In my more than four decades of priestly and episcopal ministry, the call to serve Christ and his people has taken, and continues to take, many, many forms, even as simple as answering a phone call and offering a word of consolation, congratulations, encouragement, or support. But I remind myself in those moments, the reason the phone rang in the first place was because the person who was calling wanted to speak to a priest—the person who is identified in the hearts and minds of our faithful—in the teaching and proclamation of the Church, as another Christ, *alter Christus*.

Priestly spirituality is intrinsically Eucharistic.
—Sacramentum Caritatis *80*

At each meeting of the Priests Council I like to begin with a reading, usually from one of Saint Paul's letters, and then a brief reflection on how it relates to our ministry as priests and our work together on the council, followed by a prayer. This, I hope, reminds all of us that even in something as seemingly mundane as a meeting, we are carrying out our priestly ministry—in one of its many formats.

In the apostolic exhortation that followed on the 1990 synod on priestly formation, *Pastores Dabo Vobis*, we are taught once again of the central role of the Eucharist.

> Pastoral charity, which has its specific source in the sacrament of holy orders, finds its full expression and its supreme nourishment in the Eucharist. As the Council states: "This pastoral charity flows mainly from the eucharistic sacrifice, which is thus the center and root of the whole priestly life. The priestly soul strives thereby to apply to itself the action which takes place on the altar of sacrifice." (*PO* 14, *PD* 23)

At the altar in the midst of the eucharistic liturgy, we priests are extraordinarily blessed to know who we are, what we are called to make present today, and how that very action is the source of our new life in Christ as his priests. When asked what identifies diocesan priestly spirituality, I think the answer is a very simple one: *we are called to make Christ present in his word and in the sacraments.* The crowning of this memorializing action is the Eucharist—the Mass. To the extent that we open ourselves as fully as we can to Christ working in and through us, to that extent does our spiritual life draw nourishment and flourish.

Holy Uselessness
Rev. Msgr. J. Wilfrid Parent

As a parish priest, I try to draw people to the Eucharist. And so, I have worked hard for better worship at Mass—better music, better environments, better lay participation, better preaching, and so on.

Yet I sometimes wonder if I have been too focused on making the Eucharist *useful*—useful in the sense that the experience is sufficiently pleasant to keep people in the pews. In a consumer culture like ours, working for better worship can easily become just another consumer enterprise, where the Eucharist is measured by its Sunday ratings.

How many saints have advanced along the way of perfection thanks to their Eucharistic devotion! . . . Holiness has always found its center in the sacrament of the Eucharist.
—Sacramentum Caritatis 94

At such times, I am haunted by the purity of Christ's sacrifice. As Jesus bled out his life on the cross, we were utterly useless to him. He revealed that to love someone means to release that person from the tyranny of usefulness—from the expectation that he or she exists to fulfill *my* worldly needs and desires.

The moment that we demand that the Eucharist *must* fulfill another purpose—the moment we say that it *must* be pleasant or *must* fulfill any worldly need is the moment that we do not really love God but are trying to use him.

The measure of authentic worship seems to me to be the degree to which we are willing to be useless for God. We are "useless" in a worldly sense when we feed the hungry who will never be able to repay us, care for the sick who will only die, or forgive enemies who will continue to hate us. I find the silence of eucharistic adoration an especially fruitful source of such holy uselessness.

While I still work hard to make worship at Mass useful, I also work to avoid the tyranny of usefulness through useless acts of love, which is the essence of Christ's eucharistic sacrifice.

The Eucharist Strengthens Us in Difficult Times
Most Rev. John B. McCormack

Since boyhood, I have been drawn to visit the Lord, present in the Blessed Sacrament, especially when I felt in need of help. I was able to do this regularly since my family home was near our parish church and there was always a chapel in the schools I attended. As you might imagine, it was not long before I found myself visiting the Lord often as the crisis surrounding the sexual abuse of children by some priests unfolded.

Faith in and love for the Eucharist cannot allow Christ's presence in the tabernacle to remain alone.
—John Paul II[16]

For several years, I was involved as a priest in pastorally responding to victims, their families, and the accused priests. In later years, as a bishop, I have had the responsibility to help all members of the diocese deal with their upset, embarrassment, and sometimes their disillusionment with the Church and with me concerning these horrific events. I was singled out in the media as someone particularly to blame. This was very painful. As time passed, I wondered how I could ever help others, or even myself, find the strength needed.

As I emptied my heart to Christ in prayer before the Blessed Sacrament, I became more aware that he would lead the faithful and me through this. I felt comforted and strengthened by his eucharistic presence. The Eucharist reminds me of how suffering is transformed by love. Christ was made perfect through his suffering on the cross. Like the grain of wheat, Jesus died so that we might be nourished and live in his love. Through the love I experienced in the Eucharist, I knew he was helping me die to self and live for others.

I know that I would not have been able to keep moving forward in my life and ministry without personally knowing his love for me and for everyone. Praying to Christ present in the Blessed Sacrament, especially during these difficult times, has drawn me closer to him. His eucharistic presence has given me strength.

Through the cross of these days, I have tasted the humility of our crucified Lord and his compassionate love for his people. Coming to believe more fully in His presence in the Eucharist and in other people, whether faithful friends or constant critics, has truly become a joy for me. It has been a time of great suffering for many, and for me, but I have found it also to be a unique time of grace.

For this I am deeply grateful.

COMMUNION IN A FRACTURED WORLD
Rev. Anthony Oelrich

⸻

I recently came across a marvelous description of the Church. The Church is the place of "the dynamic movement of gathering" first begun in Christ.[1]

The reality of gathering expresses for me something very powerful about the Eucharist. While presiding one Sunday morning at St. Mary's Cathedral, this was brought home to me in a concrete way. Standing before me was an amazing mixture of people. Ethnically, politically, economically, theologically, people of many types and on every place of the spectrum, responded to my "The Lord be with you," as one, "And also with you." As the one bread and the one cup are transformed into the living presence of Christ, all these different people enter into that one life of Christ. From such difference, unity is made possible.

If celebrated in a faith-filled and attentive way, Mass is formative in the deepest sense of the word, since it fosters the priest's configuration to Christ and strengthens him in his vocation.
—Sacramentum Caritatis 94

The daily Eucharist reminds me of this when I pray, "Grant that we, who are nourished by his body and blood, may be filled with his Holy Spirit, and become one body, one spirit in Christ" (Eucharistic Prayer III). The Eucharist is that place where the Spirit is powerfully acting to continue the dynamic movement of gathering people into Christ.

Our world is marked by much division, enormous economic gaps, and by separations of fear and misunderstanding. In the Eucharist, I experience God not simply breaking down the barriers and closing the gaps, but gathering us with all our differences into a unity that only God is big enough to sustain and somehow transform.

In my priesthood, too, where I often feel pulled in so many directions, I am called to be many different things to different people. The daily celebration of the Eucharist is where I find Christ gathering me back together and showing me that he is big enough for all the diverse needs of the people.

For me, the Eucharist is the encounter with the possibility of communion in a complicated, often fractured world.

The Pearl of Great Price

Rev. David L. Toups

―――

The kingdom of heaven is like a merchant
searching for fine pearls.
When he finds a pearl of great price,
he goes and sells all that he has and buys it.
—Matthew 13:45–46

―――

This parable took on a deeper personal meaning for me during
a thirty-day Ignatian retreat a number of years ago. During a
silent retreat of such length, everything is heard with new ears. The
readings at Mass spoke to me profoundly during those sacred days.
I was interiorly moved as the parable of the
"pearl of great price" was proclaimed one day, *I looked down*
and I continued to ponder it throughout the *and realized that,*
liturgy. As the ciborium was passed to the *indeed, I was holding*
concelebrants during the Lamb of God, I took *"the pearl of great*
a small, round host and placed it in the palm *price," Jesus Christ.*
of my hand.

Now this may not sound unusual, but as most priests are used
to being the principal celebrant, a larger host is generally used;
thus the small round white host in my palm was not a familiar
sight. Eyes watering, I looked down and realized that, indeed, I was
holding "the pearl of great price," Jesus Christ, for whom, as his
priest, I had given everything. Here was the treasure, the glorious
gift of God, the precious and beautiful eucharistic Lord of heaven
and earth that priests are privileged to hold in their hands every

day. This may not seem striking. Periodically, it would be perfectly reasonable to be moved to tears by lifting up bread and bringing down God. I do not, however, have the "gift of tears." When I find myself welling up, it is indeed a movement of the Holy Spirit. This moment was not so much a conversion, because I never doubted the eucharistic presence, but rather a deeper interiorization of the truth. That day the Lord drew me into a more profound relationship with his eucharistic presence and appreciation for the gift of priesthood.

Gift Transcending All Fullness[18]

In the eyes of the world, priests seem to have sacrificed everything with little or no compensation. Yet the parable of the "pearl of great price" speaks to this, selling all to possess what is most important. Granted we do not "possess" Christ but are rather possessed by him and given so much in return. The words of Saint Paul ring true, "We seem to have nothing, yet everything is ours" (2 Cor 6:10). In Jesus Christ, in the eucharistic celebration of the Catholic faith, we have found the "pearl of great price,"

In the eucharistic celebration of the Catholic faith, we have found the "pearl of great price."

which gives meaning to whatever sacrifices we are asked to offer. The pearl comes at a price, but "where there is love, sacrifice is easy," as stated in the vocation's video *Fishers of Men*.[19] Even Saint Peter asked Our Lord:

> We have given up everything and followed you. What will there be for us? Jesus said to them, ". . . everyone who has given up houses or brothers or sisters or father or mother or children or lands for the sake of my name will receive a hundred times more, and will inherit eternal life." (Mt 19:27, 29)

Every priest knows the beauty of participating in the lives of so many families. To be a spiritual father is at the heart of the rewarding and life-giving nature of the priesthood. To share the "pearl of great price" with others is the *raison d'être* of the priest. The late Pope John Paul II described his priestly vocation as a "gift and mystery"; that day on retreat I recognized anew the awesome "gift and mystery" of the vocation to which I also have been called.[20]

MYSTERY OF FAITH

The Lord Jesus has chosen priests to be the instrument of divine grace through which he manifests himself to his faithful flock. Indeed, we who stand *in persona Christi capitis* have been given the privilege to invite the eucharistic Lord to the altar every day. Nourishing the family of faith in word and sacrament as a spiritual father is a source of great contentment and joy. Vatican II reminds the whole Church that the Divine Liturgy is the "source and summit" of our faith. But at times, this great ritual can become rote; going through the motions can become an occupational hazard. Thus daily personal reflection upon what we are doing at each Mass and who it is that we hold in our hands—*mysterium fidei*—is of great importance. After all, it is not just about a rite; it is about a relationship: a relationship with Jesus, the Good Shepherd, who has called us to help feed his flock just as he called the first apostles: "Do this in memory of me" (Lk 22:19). Pope Benedict XVI reminds us priests:

Nourishing the family of faith is a source of great contentment and joy.

> It is impossible to receive the Lord every day, taking his Body and Blood into our hands, pronouncing the tremendous and wonderful words: "This is my Body, this is my Blood" without letting ourselves be seized by him, without letting ourselves be won over by fascination for him, without letting his infinite love change us from within.[21]

Bond of Charity

As one of the junior authors in this book, a priest of the so-called "JPII Generation," I feel it important to say "thank you" to my older brothers in the priesthood. We would not be ordained today if not for your priestly ministry to us and to our families. We acknowledge that we come from our own unique periods of history and, at times, there are generational gaps. We certainly did not experience the tumultuous years after the Council. But now we are brothers in the ministry, and we are "in the trenches" together. We need you to mentor us, to offer us a good example, to be our brothers.

Not coming from the same school of thought often presents relational obstacles, so let us find our source of unity in the Eucharist, as St. Augustine eloquently preached: "O *The vast majority* Sacrament of Love! O Sign of Unity! O Bond *of priests find* of Charity!"[22] Studies show that the vast *great fulfillment* majority of priests find great fulfillment in *in celebrating the* celebrating the sacraments.[23] May we find joy *sacraments.* together in the bond of unity so that, as a united presbyterate, we may be a more efficacious sign of Christ's love through our fraternity. As brothers, we need each other. Let us listen to Saint Paul's counsel:

> Put on then, as God's chosen ones, holy and beloved, heartfelt compassion, kindness, humility, gentleness, and patience, bearing with one another and forgiving one another, if one has a grievance against another; as the Lord has forgiven you, so must you also do. And over all these put on love, that is, the bond of perfection. And let the peace of Christ control your hearts, the peace into which you were also called in one body. And be thankful. (Col 3:12–15)

Tremendous and Life-Giving Sacrament

The liturgy, as handed on by the Church, always has deep relevance. While our cultural enthusiasm for what is new might lead us to make innovations in the liturgy, it would be a mistake to go beyond the liturgical norms. The Mass should be a familiar and comfortable place to *rest on the bosom of the Lord*, like John at the Last Supper. The liturgy is a place for all of the faithful to feel at home without having to guess what might happen next. In a word, the Mass is a place where Jesus comes to us at every celebration despite how we feel, the effectiveness of our preaching, or the quality of the music. This should be a great comfort to us and to every Catholic who understands the reality of the Eucharist. That is not to say that the subjective dynamics of the liturgy are not important. We need always prepare our preaching well and allocate resources so that the sacred music elevates the hearts of believers. It would be irresponsible on the part of pastors to ignore these important factors. But the Mass is always the Mass. For the priest it is not about his preferences but about true

Jesus comes to us at every celebration despite how we feel.

leitourgia—a service for the people of God. He is to be "all things to all" people (1 Cor 9:22), while remaining ever-faithful to the Church.

The priest is the servant of the liturgy because he is the servant of Christ and of the Church. To say, "I don't say Mass for *that* group" is to cease being a servant. Whether in a parish or a convent, in a charismatic community or at a Latin Mass, at a youth Mass or at the rectory alone on one's day off,[24] every day this is the opportunity to encounter "the pearl of great price." The Mass is to be loved and celebrated carefully and with reverent devotion in every community in which the priest finds himself. It is the "essential moment of their day" (*PD* 48). It is the tremendous and life-giving Sacrament.

Most High and Adorable Sacrament

Christ loves his Church so much that he is not only present to us in the celebration but he remains with us for adoration. As a young seminarian, I listened to a taped lecture by the late Archbishop Fulton Sheen speaking about his daily holy hour before the tabernacle. He said:

> We become like that which we gaze upon. Looking into a sunset, the face takes on a golden glow. Looking at the eucharistic Lord for an hour transforms the heart in a mysterious way as the face of Moses was transformed after his companionship with God on the mountain.[25]

I was so inspired by this oration that, almost twenty years later, I faithfully continue to follow this practice. Adoration, as the extension of the Mass, keeps us grounded in the intimate relationship that the Lord desires for each of his children, and especially his priests. It keeps us focused through our struggles, heals our wounded hearts, comforts us in sorrow, and accompanies us in the joys of priestly life and ministry.

Adoration, as the extension of the Mass, keeps us grounded in the intimate relationship that the Lord desires.

During this daily "radiation therapy," God can work on us in ways which only he is aware. Pope Benedict XVI recently stated that the priest's life "must be nourished with assiduous prayer." He went on to encourage priests:

> Be models of prayer, become masters of prayer. May your days be marked by times of prayer, during which, after Jesus' example, you engage in a regenerating conversation with the Father. I know it is not easy to stay faithful to this daily appointment with the Lord, especially today when the pace of life is frenetic and worries absorb us more and more. Yet we must convince ourselves: the time he spends in prayer is the most important time in a priest's life, in which divine grace acts with greater

effectiveness, making his ministry fruitful . . . time for prayer must be given a true priority in our life.[26]

O come let us adore him!

REFRESHMENT OF HOLY SOULS

Although not a norm or obligation like the Divine Office, times of personal prayer are highly beneficial to our spiritual lives. I am not going to pretend that this hour is always easy. In fact, for men this lack of *doing* can be particularly difficult. For me, prayer has to come from two avenues: grace and discipline. Prayer is a gift, but without availing myself to God by scheduling time (i.e., discipline), it would never happen. In preparation for the thirty-day retreat, I asked a wise and holy spiritual director what I should be praying for, and the response was, "Marian receptivity." At the time, I thought this was hokey. It made no sense to me until I entered into the intensity of the retreat—four to five hours of spiritual exercises a day. Then I realized that I needed to be more receptive and open to the Holy Spirit in order to pray. At this point I began to panic (realizing that there were twenty-nine days left!) and begged God for the grace to have a heart like Mary, open to "receive" in silent union with him. With heart opened before the presence of Christ in the tabernacle, slowly prayer began to open up as my posture became more helpless and receptive: "God, I can't do this, but you can!" The retreat unfolded with many graces, but without the disposition of Marian receptivity, this could never have happened. It often still goes against the grain of my masculine sense of *doing*, but I know that without daily surrender I will not grow in intimacy with the Lord.

The daily holy hour has been evermore a time of refreshment: union with God. Marian receptivity now makes sense as I pray to be ever more open to divine love. Part of the *cost* of the "pearl of great price" is the death of what I desire; dying to *doing*. I am

> *For me, prayer has to come from two avenues: grace and discipline.*

growing in my understanding of *doing*. Less is actually more. During my time of prayer each day, I strive to keep at least half an hour to simply *being* with God. I might have begun with one of the hours of the Office, some spiritual reading or a Rosary, but the time for intimate silence is the real key. As Blessed Teresa of Calcutta would often say, "In the silence of the heart, God speaks." Indeed, I have found this to be true for my spiritual life. And on those days when my mind is swimming with thoughts of undone work, the sacred scriptures "prime the pump" of my soul and offer a focus for that time of silence through simple *lectio divina*.

In a homily to his former congregation, Pope Benedict XVI said, "Silence and contemplation have a purpose: they serve, in the distractions of daily life, to preserve permanent union with God. This is their purpose: that union with God may always be present in our souls and may transform our entire being."[27] Silence before the tabernacle allows me to be receptive to what God wants to do in and through me, and less what I want to do for God. It is all grace, but discipline is still necessary in that I make time for God. The two most important moments of my day are the celebration of the Mass and the eucharistic holy hour. They are the *sine qua non* of my life.

> Nothing more difficult nor more dangerous can happen to a man than to hold in his hands and bring to be, through his words, him whom the angels, so far beyond our conception and praise, cannot comprehend or sufficiently extol.
> —Saint Francis de Sales[28]

Medicine of Immortality, Viaticum of Those Who Die in the Lord, Pledge of Future Glory

Just one year after my re-discovery of the "pearl of great price," I was taken deeper once again by the Lord. My father, who taught me how to be a father, was being led by Jesus to the house of *the* Father. Confined to bed and ravaged by cancer, this once virile man was weak and emaciated. With deep gratitude, he watched me prepare a makeshift altar in his bedroom in the presence of my mother, brother, and sister. Although he was barely able to speak, he communicated his gratitude for the gift of the Mass about to be celebrated. He always loved going to *his son's* Mass (he was the president of my fan club!). This time was not different, but now he knew that he would soon be seeing the Lord face to face. As the Mass unfolded, the gospel of the day was from Saint John:

> Whoever eats on my flesh and drinks my blood has eternal life, and I will raise him up on the last day. For my flesh is true food and my blood true drink. Whoever eats my flesh and drinks my blood remains in me and I in him. (Jn 6:54–56)

As I proclaimed the Lord's words, I looked at my dad, the first to lead me to the Eucharist. He knew this "Medicine of Immortality" from my hand would soon lead him to eternal life. No longer able to eat, he was being fed. I had received flesh from him, now his own flesh wasted, he looked to me for Flesh that would raise him up. What a mystery; *Viaticum*—Christ, food for the journey. Gathered around the sanctuary of his bed, my family and I were consoled by the words of Jesus: "Whoever eats on my flesh and drinks my blood has eternal life, and I will raise him up on the last day." No bright cathedral celebration could compare to that day in the small, dimly-lit room around my father's sickbed. There are times when words do not avail, when the word of God and the Bread of Life alone can touch and heal. There was not a dry eye in the room, not even mine.

No bright cathedral celebration could compare to that day in the small, dimly-lit room around my father's sickbed.

My father was dying. I was there as his son and his priest. In the act of handing over my father, finally and fully, into eternal life, my eyes were once again opened to the gift from my hands, the Bread of Life. What a price. What a pearl! "When he finds a pearl of great price, he goes and sells all that he has and buys it." What a gift to have been called to be an instrument of Christ in the world—what a life, and it is yours O priest of Jesus Christ.

ABSOLUTE TRANSCENDENT MYSTERY
Rev. Benedict J. Groeschel, C.F.R.

———

Like most Catholics of the pre-Vatican II era, I understood that the Eucharist was the presence of Christ with me—the real presence. The Mass, Benediction, Forty Hours, processions, visits to the Blessed Sacrament— all these emphasized that our Lord was with me in my daily life. This sense of the divine presence did not change when liturgical theology refocused my attention on the Eucharist as sacrament and sacrifice. These teachings all came together and complemented each other. However, in recent years the Eucharist has come to mean something else for me—a focus on mystery, which invites me into the infinite and the transcendent.

Surprisingly, the person who opened this door for me was Albert Einstein, who defined the mystical as the perception of a reality that we cannot understand or comprehend. I have learned from independent sources that the greatest scientist in history loved to talk with Catholic priests about the Eucharist and about the "luminous figure of Christ."

I can only speculate that Saint Thomas' theology of transubstantiation fitted in with Einstein's theory of matter. When one

If anything could shake my faith in the Eucharist it would not be the doubt as to how the bread could become flesh . . . but if I ask myself how he could love us so much as to make himself our food, I can only answer that this is a mystery of faith.
—St. Alphonsus Liguori[29]

ponders these two theoretical explorations into the mysterious nature of matter, there are obvious similarities.

Every day Christ's eucharistic sacrifice puts us in touch with absolute transcendent mystery. It opens our feeble human thoughts to the reality of that which never changes and has no limitations: the mystery of God.

The Eucharist also draws us into the most profound mystery of God, namely, the mystery of redeeming love through sacrifice and total dedication. The Eucharist proclaims the mystery of the God who dies, who experiences human suffering and death out of love. In the Mass, I am confronted with a God who reaches out to me with wounded human hands.

If I really think about the question, "What does the Eucharist mean to me?" I must ultimately respond, "It means everything."

Never Far From Home
Rev. Timothy A. Butler, U.S.A.F.

In the fall of 1967, I received my first Holy Communion. I now qualified to be an altar server. Because my Dad was a humble milkman, we could not afford to buy a cassock and surplice. The sacristan at our parish, a relation, knew I wanted to do this more than anything. So she searched through the closets in the sacristy, found an old abandoned set, and fixed it up for me. I was ecstatic.

As a new altar server, I was assigned to the 6:00 a.m. daily Mass before school. There, in the semi-darkness of morning, I experienced the presence of God. Even at this young age, I knew it as a twofold reality. Jesus was as clearly present in the Blessed Sacrament in the tabernacle as he was in the people gathered, quietly saying their Rosary in the candlelight as I set up the altar and devoutly joining in the prayers of the Mass. My experience of God's presence during those early morning Masses left an emotional fingerprint on me that has been a touchstone throughout my life.

This presence has been particularly important to me as a military chaplain. Our military community is highly mobile. We are transferred to new assignments every couple of years, often to foreign countries, and usually to austere locations, in support of military operations. Far away from home, Mass is often the only "place" that is familiar. Whether celebrated on the hood of a Humvee, in a tent, on board a ship, out in the field, or in one of our chapels, there is a presence there, God's presence, in the people gathered and in the bread and wine we share. In the midst of the unfamiliar, Eucharist alone reminds us that we are never far from home.

> Altar servers see you at the regular Sunday and weekday celebrations; in your hands they see the Eucharist "take place." On your face they see its mystery reflected; and in your heart they sense the summons of a greater love. May you be for them fathers, teachers and witnesses of Eucharistic piety and holiness of life!
> —John Paul II
> Holy Thursday Letter, 2004

A Few Thoughts on the Eucharist
Cardinal Carlo Maria Martini, S.J.

———

Some of my brothers have the habit of keeping an account of the Masses that they have celebrated, beginning with their ordination, in order to reconstruct the preordained time for their first privileged eucharistic moment. I never felt this need because it has always seemed to me that in one Mass there would be all Masses and what counted was not the number but one's interior devotion. Thank God, having completed fifty-six years of priesthood, there has been granted to me the gift of celebrating the Eucharist almost every day and, often, many times a day—without ever taking these rituals for granted, but experiencing a new appreciation each time.

Naturally, I ought to speak about what the eucharistic presence in the tabernacle means to me. I discovered it in all its power when I was about eleven years old, praying in a church in the mountains before a tabernacle where there was a lit candle. The thought that there was a living presence within that tabernacle made a great impression on me, and I spent a long time in prayer. From that time, in order to find my bearings in a given location, I keep in mind the places where the Most Blessed Sacrament is kept. On some trips abroad, I recall the pain I experienced while thinking that within the range of a few kilometers, even in a large city, the presence of Jesus in the Eucharist did not exist.

But above all, I am thankful for the great gift which has been given me of not ever taking the Mass for granted, but finding again and again the newness of its mystery. The Vatican II reforms have been easy for me to accept because they corresponded with my experience. I truly hope that there will not be any turning back from that maturity in understanding the Eucharist reached in the Church, especially in *Sacrosanctum Concilium.*

Certainly the liturgical reform inaugurated by the Council has greatly contributed to a more conscious, active and fruitful participation in the Holy Sacrifice of the Altar on the part of the faithful.
—Ecclesia de Eucharistia *10*

THE EUCHARIST: A CALL TO PRIESTLY HOLINESS

Rev. Msgr. Stephen J. Rossetti

———

R ecently, I traveled to a diocese for its annual convocation of priests. It was a several day affair and the subject of the convocation was the health and welfare of priests today. We spoke together about the many challenges of priesthood in our current climate and the ways in which priests cope with these challenges. At one point, the subject of the Eucharist arose. When the priests began speaking about the Eucharist, they became noticeably energized and upbeat. They began to speak from the heart and shared in touching and poignant ways.

When the priests began speaking about the Eucharist, they became noticeably energized and upbeat.

Several of the older priests said that the Mass had become the center of their lives. They spoke about how meaningful the eucharistic celebration with the people had become. Many said that Mass had become even more personally important down through the years. It was striking and uplifting to hear how central the Eucharist was to these fine priests. Clearly, the Eucharist had an increasingly deep meaning for them.

It was good for me and for all of us in the room to hear their profound words. We priests are not good about sharing our souls with each other. We keep our spiritual lives largely hidden from others, including our brother priests. We rarely speak about our personal relationships with the Lord, what priesthood means to us, or about such intimate spiritual realities as the Eucharist.

Our lives as priests are certainly not superficial or boring. They are filled with intense pastoral encounters on a daily basis. We regularly enter the sacred places in others. And each day our souls are touched profoundly in many ways, especially at the Lord's table. What a blessed life we have! But it seems to me we keep our spiritual riches hidden.

And at the center of this priestly life is the Eucharist. I think we would be further nourished and strengthened if we were able to speak, at appropriate moments, about such things to our brothers in the priesthood, and beyond. Many others, including potential vocations to the priesthood, would also be encouraged and strengthened if they were to hear what is in the hearts of our priests. *I continue to maintain that one of the most well-guarded secrets in our church today is the depth of meaning and heartfelt joy of a priestly life.* And at the center of this priestly life is the Eucharist.

A Priest Is More Than a Presider

When we speak of the priest at the Eucharist, we often speak of him as the "presider." This is certainly true. He does indeed "preside" as the "General Instruction of the Roman Missal" noted. As such, he is the "president" of the assembly. But he is more.

As the "General Instruction" noted, "For the celebration of the Eucharist is an action of the whole Church" (GIRM 5) and thus, it is a sacramental action in which the whole community actively participates. Nevertheless, the role of the priest is unique. The "General Instruction" goes on to say:

> At the Last Supper Christ instituted the paschal sacrifice and banquet by which the sacrifice of the cross is continuously made present in the Church whenever the priest, representing Christ the Lord, carries out what the

Lord himself did and handed over to his disciples to be
done in his memory. (GIRM 72)

It is clear that the Eucharist is more than a remote reminder
of something that happened long ago. Rather, something dynamic
happens at each Eucharist—the sacrifice of the cross is "made present." And the role of the priest is pivotal. While Christ is present in
the entire assembly, there can be no Eucharist without the priest.

The priest does more than preside over the sacrament. In the
Eucharist, he, who stands in the person of Christ and has been
uniquely configured to him, enters into the death and resurrection
of Christ as the sacrifice of the cross is made present. This is one of
the reasons why communion
services, in the absence of a
priest, are good but cannot take
the place of the eucharistic sacrifice. In the former, the faithful
are blessed to receive the previously consecrated eucharistic
species. But in the Mass, the
original sacrifice itself is dynam-
ically present.

It is in the very person of
Jesus that the paschal sacrifice—his
passion, death, and resurrection—
brings salvation to the world. In
the sacrifice of the Mass, Jesus
is present in the entire assembly,
but most especially in the person of the priest. Why is it that
the priest prays the words of
consecration in the first person:
"This is *my* body and this is *my*
blood"? It is Christ who speaks in him and, once again, his body
and blood poured out on the cross, are at hand. The priest himself
is sacramentally immolated to the measure that Christ dwells in

> As ministers of sacred
> realities, especially in
> the Sacrifice of the
> Mass, priests represent
> the person of Christ in
> a special way. He gave
> Himself as a victim to
> make men holy. Hence
> priests are invited to
> imitate the realities they
> deal with. Since they
> celebrate the mystery
> of the Lord's death,
> they should see to it
> that every part of their
> being is dead to evil
> habits and desires.
> —*Presbyterorum
> Ordinis* 13

him. There can be no Eucharist without the priest. And he, too, mounts the wood of the cross, in a sacramental way, as he ascends to the altar.

With such a realization, any functional notion of the priesthood evaporates quickly, and the grandeur of the priesthood shines forth. If we think of the Mass as simply something the priests *does*, as a function that he performs, then we have misunderstood the depths of the divine mysteries present in the sacraments and the depth of the priestly life. I suspect we have all unintentionally fallen prey, at times, to this limited functional notion of priesthood.

The priest himself is sacramentally immolated to the measure that Christ dwells in him.

Perhaps we continually fall into functionalism because the grandeur of the priestly calling is beyond comprehension. But this should not be a great surprise, since we priests are only mirroring the unfathomable depths of the mystery of Christ, who remains beyond human comprehension. How could anyone fully understand his mystery, and thus our own mystery? While we should always strive to penetrate these depths, we do so only feebly.

Such depths are perhaps best understood by our more senior priests, those who, as noted earlier, spoke about their increasingly deep personal bond with the Eucharist and its increasing centrality in their lives. It may be that, over the years, they have come to experience more deeply the mystery of their calling and of Christ, which ultimately remains beyond the capacity of human words to express. If we do not express it well or much, it may be because it is beyond the realm of full human cognition. But they have seen it "indistinctly, as in a mirror" (1 Cor 13:12).

We have an important theological notion, *ex opere operato*, meaning that the grace of the sacrament is conferred regardless of the sanctity of the priest. One can readily see how pastorally important this notion is. The grace of Christ is given through the hands of his ministers, but transcends their personal limitations. This rightly places the primacy of the action in the person of Christ, not in his ministers.

Nevertheless, at times, we may have exaggerated our application of this valid theological concept. The integrity and sanctity of our priests are not something extraneous to the efficacy of his priestly ministry. He is not simply someone who dispenses gifts from God without being involved in the gift. Rather, he himself participates in the mysteries since it is Christ, in him, who is acting through his total person.

Thus, the integrity and sanctity of the priest are important. While the sacrament will be conferred regardless, it is time to look more closely at the role of the person of the priest in whom Christ is acting. We are all aware of the great good that one priest can do; witness the ministry of the saintly Curé of Ars in a remote village in France. We have also recently witnessed what great harm a priest can do when his actions are scandalous. As Pope Benedict XVI said on the eve of his 2008 pastoral visit to the United States, "It is more important to have good priests than to have many priests." *The sanctity of our priests is not a peripheral matter.*

THE PRIEST TOO IS TAKEN UP IN SACRIFICE

While the Sacrifice of the Mass is the work of Christ, it is accomplished through very human people, the people assembled and most centrally, the priest. The priest, as noted previously, is not only the instrument of this sacramental grace. He too, in the person of Christ, offers himself in the sacrifice. So too, the people gathered, "they should give thanks to God; by offering the Immaculate Victim, not only through the hands of the priest, but also with him, they should learn also to offer themselves" (*SC* 48).

The sanctity of our priests is not a peripheral matter.

The offering of the priest and the people is not incidental to the Mass. Therefore, the Council Fathers of Vatican II noted in *Presbyterorum Ordinis*:

> Thus when priests join in the act of Christ the Priest, they offer themselves entirely to God, and when they are nourished with the body of Christ they profoundly share in the love of him who gives himself as food to the faithful. In like fashion they are united with the intention and love of Christ when they administer the sacraments. (*PO* 13)

The priest is not only presiding at the offering of Christ, he is united to Christ in love, and he offers himself with Christ's sacrifice in this action. He not only is the instrument through which the paschal mystery is made present, he enters into the mystery itself.

The saints and mystics often give us examples of truths that we profess, but are hidden from our daily experience. For example, in the recently canonized Padre Pio of Pietrelcina, we have a striking example of a priest-celebrant who seemed to enter fully into the paschal mystery at the altar. Those who witnessed Padre Pio celebrating Mass were often deeply moved by the experience (see p. 123 for Msgr. Paul Lenz's experience of attending a Mass celebrated by Padre Pio). When asked about his Masses, which could last for hours, and how he could stand on his feet for so long, Padre Pio said, "I never tire of standing so long, and could not become tired, because I am not standing, but am on the cross with Christ, suffering with him."

We need to do more than act or look like priests on the outside.

Padre Pio appeared to be living the death and resurrection of Jesus while he celebrated the Mass. At times, people reported seeing signs of great sorrow, agony, and grief in his face during the Mass. He himself appeared to be going through the crucifixion of Jesus. At other times, he would be filled with joy and his face would be radiant. Regarding the Mass he said, "The holy Mass is a sacred union of Jesus and myself. I suffer unworthily all that was suffered by Jesus who deigned to allow me to share in his great enterprise of human redemption."

While Padre Pio had a unique vocation as a priest-victim, I suspect Padre Pio would agree that, for all priests, the Mass is a sacred union of Jesus and the priest. And in that union, the priest is taken up into the complete self-gift of Jesus to the Father.

A CALL TO INTEGRITY AND HOLINESS

Is the priest's remote and proximate preparation for the celebration of the Eucharist incidental to the sacrament? Is his own sanctity extraneous to the total experience of the sacrament? If he is to find himself, in Christ, on the paten and in the chalice, then the answer is obviously no. While the sacrament is efficacious, *ex opere operato*, history is replete with striking examples of what one holy priest can do, or what one priest can destroy. Again, all of us have witnessed how one fine priest can ignite the faith of an entire parish, or how one priest can quickly dismember its unity and life.

If there is any lesson that must strike us in these past few years, I think it is how important it is that we live our priestly lives with integrity. We need to do more than act or look like priests on the outside, we must also truly be priests on the inside. Lest we fall into a merely functional notion of priesthood, we ought to remind ourselves often of the truth that we must first *be* priests. We must truly say from our hearts, "This is *my* body. . . . This is *my* blood."

> Priestly holiness itself contributes very greatly to a fruitful fulfillment of the priestly ministry. True, the grace of God can complete the work of salvation even through unworthy ministers. Yet ordinarily God desires to manifest His wonders through those who have been made particularly docile to the impulse and guidance of the Holy Spirit. Because of their intimate union with Christ and their holiness of life, these men can say with the Apostle: "It is now no longer I that live, but Christ lives in me" (Gal 2:20).
> —*Presbyterorum Ordinis* 12

Only a few weeks ago, a bishop called me about one of his priests. The man had been ordained for many years. It was discovered by one of his parishioners that the man had been living a double life. He had been using cyber-porn and engaged in a number of sexual encounters. When the bishop approached the priest, the latter admitted his actions but responded with surprise, "What is the problem? I am good and kind to the people." He saw nothing wrong with his behavior and was mystified that the bishop was so upset. Sadly, some priests rose to the man's defense, despite knowing the basic facts.

We priests are being called to a level of holiness and integrity that we may not have envisioned for ourselves.

This is an extreme and distressing example of functionalism. What kind of offering is the priest making when he puts himself on the paten? What kind of gift is offered to the Father when he is united to Christ in the Mass? Surely the unseen rays of grace will be less radiant in this man's priesthood.

In my years ministering at Saint Luke Institute, I have seen the results of sin and the joy of holiness. I have spent sixteen years working with priests and religious who have become mired in a variety of personal and psychological problems. I can tell you most assuredly that sinful actions bring misery, shame, and ultimately death to one's vocation and death to one's life. It is one of the greatest tricks of Satan to make us think that sin is attractive and makes one happy. I have witnessed, time and again, that being caught up in alcohol abuse, drug addictions, stealing money, and/or immoral sexual conduct makes one miserable. The most miserable being of them all is Satan himself and his minions who live in hell.

At Saint Luke Institute, our goal is to help as many priests and religious as possible turn from the path of death to life. After a priest has finished our program, I often will sit down with him and ask, "Tell me what your life was like before you entered this place." Every alcoholic, for example, will respond, "My life was horrible. It was hell. I felt miserable about myself, and my priesthood was a shambles." "And now?" I ask him. "Tell me how you feel now that you have lived a life of sobriety for many months." He will invariably respond, "I feel good about myself. I am excited to be a priest again. I have hope for the future." "Well then," I respond, "There is your choice. Next time you feel like drinking, remember the choice you are making." Indeed, the choice is, ultimately, a choice between heaven and hell.

In the Rite of Ordination the bishop exhorts the ordinand to "believe what you read, teach what you believe, and put into practice what you teach." Essentially, we are asked to live a life of integrity. We are not only to preach and teach the gospel, we are to live it in our lives. Truly being a priest requires both.

"What kind of gift am I, being placed on that paten each day with Christ?"

The Second Vatican Council said that the priest, like all Christians, is called to holiness. However, it added that the vocation of priesthood ushers in a unique challenge and call to sanctity:

> Like all other Christians, they have received in the sacrament of Baptism the symbol and gift of such a calling and such grace that even in human weakness they can and must seek for perfection. . . . Priests are bound, however, to acquire that perfection in special fashion. (*PO* 12)

This actually is not hard to recognize. Certainly the faithful expect priests to apply themselves in a unique and direct way to living the gospels. And while all those present at the Mass offer themselves through Christ in the eucharistic sacrifice, the priest himself has a preeminent place in this self-offering, he who is uniquely configured to Christ the Head. It would only make sense that he has a special obligation to pursue a life of grace. Clearly, the fathers of the Second Vatican Council believed this to be true.

Each of us, who are priests, should ask ourselves, "What kind of gift am I, being placed on that paten each day with Christ?" "Am I striving for faithfulness and integrity?" It is no accident and it is a good thing that you and I begin each Mass asking for God's mercy.

Integrity in Great Things and Small

For most priests, integrity is not the issue. Thankfully, my experience with priests is that the strong majority are serving with faithfulness and integrity. I personally find our priests inspiring. I think of them getting up each day and responding to the never-ending flood of human needs that enters the doors of their rectories and churches. By and large, they respond with a patience and a compassion that, from a larger perspective, is a convincing witness to the presence of a special sacrament of orders as well as to the greatness of our priests.

> St. Jean Marie Vianney urges us all toward these heights of priestly sanctity, and we are happy to invite the priest of today to these heights because—though we are aware of the difficulties they encounter in their personal life and in the burdens of the ministry, though the temptations and the fatigues of some are not unknown to us—our experience also tells us of the courageous faithfulness of the great majority and the spiritual heights reached by the best.
> —*Sacerdotii Nostri Primordia* 7

As I travel from diocese to diocese and lead their annual convocations, it is very common that the bishop will stand up at some point during the week and address his priests. And the most common comment that will come from the lips of the bishop is, "Thank you." He will tell the priests how grateful he is, and how grateful the people are for all that they do. And one can readily tell that the bishop's words are true and come straight from his heart.

Nevertheless, I think that *now* is the moment when we priests are being called to a level of holiness and integrity that we may not have envisioned for ourselves. Perhaps it is because of the rising flood of materialism and secularism; or maybe it is in response to the subtle spread of violence and atheism. Whatever the cause, the world today needs most desperately the irresistible power of the Eucharist and the witness and sacrifice of holy priests.

This journey toward holiness does not always begin with the great things, but often with the small. At Saint Luke Institute, we speak of "seemingly irrelevant decisions" that are actually precursors to a relapse into destructive behavior. For example, long before the alcoholic takes a drink, he may engage in behavior that takes him down the wrong road. He may decide to buy a pack of cigarettes, but he chooses to go to a liquor store to buy them. Or he may decide to go out with some friends one evening, but chooses old drinking buddies with whom to go out. Likewise, a priest with a long history of sexual problems might decide to have private lunch with someone he finds attractive and/or to make a suggestive comment to such a person.

Thus, the Liturgy of the Hours is part of his eucharistic life.

In a similar way, priests should reflect upon the little decisions of their lives that may be "seemingly irrelevant," but that actually move them toward true lives of holiness or take them one step closer to lapsing into major difficulties. Of course, priests need to be faithful in avoiding scandalous sins. But more than that, they need to attend, each day and through the years, to living more faithfully the priestly vocation that they have received. This includes attending to the many "little" parts of priestly life that are constitutive of their vocation.

For example, in a survey I conducted of 1,286 priests from sixteen dioceses spread across the United States from 2004–2005, priests were asked how many of them pray all or most of the Liturgy of the Hours daily. Only 53 percent said yes. I was surprised at this since priests, during the rite of diaconal ordination, solemnly and publicly promise to pray the Divine Office daily. The bishop specifically asks: "Are you resolved . . . to celebrate faithfully the Liturgy of the Hours for the Church and for the whole world?" And it was the priests themselves in my survey who were reporting their omission.

I suspect one reason for this low response is the fact that we are daily pressured to lapse into an activism and/or a functionalism that squeezes out all time for this prayer of the Church, or any prayer for that matter. Sometimes functionalism results from a distorted mindset of doing over being. But at other times, it is simply the pressure of too many demands on one frail human being.

To live priesthood well is to live this sacramental brotherhood.

Nevertheless, the Liturgy of the Hours is extraneous neither to a priest's life nor to the efficacy of his daily eucharistic sacrifice. The Vatican Council said,

> Priests themselves extend to the other hours of the day the praise and thanksgiving of the eucharistic celebration in praying the Divine Office, offered in the name of the Church for all the people entrusted to their care, and indeed for the whole world. (*PO* 5)

Thus, the Liturgy of the Hours is part of his eucharistic life, which is at the center of his priesthood and of the entire Church.

Sometimes priests tell me that they do not find the Liturgy of the Hours to be personally nourishing. Indeed, as in all prayer, there are times when we are graced by special consolations. Most often, however, we steadfastly remain faithful to our spiritual practices, despite experiencing desolations or merely the humdrum of life. This is also true for husbands and wives who, at times, experience love and affection in their decades of marriage, and at other times, experience merely the daily humdrum of life, or even great desolations and trials.

It might also be said to priests who remark that the Divine Office is not personally nourishing, "Perhaps the grace of the Liturgy of the Hours is not primarily for you." The tentacles of grace of a priestly life reach well beyond his person to people known as well as people unseen, just as the grace of the Eucharist said by a priest in private, spreads throughout the Church and the world. Indeed, the bishop specifically states in the diaconate ordination rite that this obligation is "for the Church and the whole world."

It may appear to some priests who, at busy moments, elect not to say the Divine Office that this is a "seemingly irrelevant decision" to one's priestly integrity. But the little decisions of each day mount up over time and send us in a vector in one direction or another. The Liturgy of the Hours is just one example. But there are many more aspects, when put together, that make up a priestly life of holiness and integrity.

PRIESTLY UNITY, OBEDIENCE, AND SIMPLE LIVING

Indeed, there are many other elements to a priest's calling that have not been named yet that are also integral to him living his vocation with integrity. I mention only three: priestly unity, obedience to one's bishop, and living simply. I picked these because they pertain directly to the choices a priest makes in how he lives his life.

The eucharistic communion must include our communion with the successors of the apostles.

First, priestly unity is also not accidental to the essence of the priesthood. We are not ordained into a private practice, such as that of a lawyer or a doctor or a psychologist. We are ordained into a presbyterate gathered around the person of the bishop. As the Vatican II documents noted, "Priests by virtue of their ordination to the priesthood are united among themselves in an intimate sacramental brotherhood" (*PO* 8).

Problems that priests often suffer, which bring them to Saint Luke Institute for healing, very commonly have isolation and disconnection at their roots. The "lone ranger" priest who is separated from his brother priests, and often the people as well, is set up for a disaster. Part of the cure for the maladies that such priests suffer (alcoholism, depression, drug abuse, or sexual acting out) almost always includes reconnection. We help them to reconnect in a chaste way with others and especially their brother priests. They must develop life-giving and nourishing, chaste relationships. How can anyone live well in our intense and demanding environment today without the support of others?

To live priesthood well is to live this sacramental brotherhood. For example, the Council Fathers of Vatican II urged priests, young and old, to minister together in harmony:

> Older priests, therefore, should receive younger priests as true brothers and help them in their first undertakings and priestly duties. The older ones should likewise endeavor to understand the mentality of younger priests, even though it be different from their own. . . . By the same token, young priests should respect the age and experience of their seniors; they should seek their advice and willingly cooperate with them in everything that pertains to the care of souls. (*PO* 8)

We work together and we socialize together. We attend priestly gatherings and perhaps even belong to a priest support group as well. We have a special solicitude for those among us who are sick or struggling. And when our brother priests pass on to the Lord, we bury them with reverence and pray for their souls. Fostering priestly unity in the whole of the presbyterate, and in one's own priestly life in particular, is important.

Living simply is actually part of a much larger priestly attitude.

Second, obedience to one's bishop is integral to priesthood. In the Rite of Ordination itself we solemnly and publicly promised obedience when the bishop asked, "Do you promise respect and obedience to me and my successors?" As different bishops come and go, the priest will have different human feelings toward each one, as is expected. But the priest's obedience is one way that he remains connected to the body of the priesthood gathered around its bishop. As Vatican II wrote, "Priests, never losing sight of the fullness of the priesthood which the bishops enjoy, must respect in them the authority of Christ, the Supreme Shepherd. They must therefore stand by their bishops in sincere charity and obedience" (*PO* 7).

At Saint Luke Institute, I have seen more than a few priests who come with serious authority issues and have difficulty dealing in a balanced and healthy way with superiors. They struggle with the ability to trust. Some priests begin to veer away from our ecclesial communion, espousing their own beliefs and believing that they have come to the real "truth." This represents a significant obstacle to living priesthood well. And when such priests come to the eucharistic table, the communion that is to be celebrated and nourished has already been fractured.

The eucharistic communion must include our communion with the successors of the apostles and their priest-collaborators, our brothers. The symbol of the bishop celebrating the Mass surrounded by his priests, especially at such solemn moments as the Chrism Mass, or at priestly ordinations, for example, is a powerful one. It is a moment at which every priest should endeavor to be present. His presence not only strengthens the presbyterate and the local church, it strengthens his own priestly life as well.

The priest at the altar dies and rises, in a sacramental way, with Jesus.

Third, living simply is also a part of our priestly call. While diocesan priests do not take a vow of poverty, it is crucial that priests live simply, as the gospel calls us to do. And while all Christians are called to live simply, the priest's life is particularly and uniquely dedicated to the work of the gospel.

Some priests, who come to us at Saint Luke Institute in need of care, have gotten themselves tied up in unseemly and even scandalous behaviors. These can begin with, or may be fueled by, an inordinate love of material things such as expensive cars, lavishly decorated rectories, sumptuous meals, or other excessive sensual delights. While we can take appropriate pleasure in the things that God has made, they ought never to obscure, in our eyes and in our priestly lives, the God who made them.

Living simply, while seemingly a small decision, is actually part of a much larger priestly attitude and spirituality. Ultimately, we are men of God whose lives need to be focused on God. He must be first; the things of this world are not. And, as the years pass, we increasingly desire only to do his will, whatever that might be.

When we choose to step beyond simple living, we have made what appears to be a seemingly irrelevant decision, but which, in the end, will damage our priestly integrity.

The Eucharist Makes Us Holy

When a priest presides at the eucharistic sacrifice, he does so neither as a distant observer nor even as a mere instrument through which God's grace is bestowed. As one who is uniquely configured to Christ, he himself enters into the sacred mysteries. The eucharistic action is dynamic and alive; it is no mere remembrance of some event long ago. While the grace of the sacrament is given *ex opere operato*, it would be the extreme of functionalism to dismiss the person of the priest as irrelevant.

Priestly unity is not accidental to the essence of the priesthood.

Like the people, the priest himself is on the paten and in the chalice. And like Christ, who speaks and acts through him at the Mass, the priest is taken up into his saving actions. Thus we can say that the priest at the altar dies and rises, in a sacramental way, with Jesus. It is thus truly proper for the priest to say, "This is my body. . . . This is my blood," since he speaks in the person of Christ the head of the Church. And this entering into the life of Christ is not incidental to the eucharistic celebration but is an integral part of its sacramental action.

The inescapable conclusion is that you and I, my brothers in the priesthood, have been given an inestimable gift. Much has been written about this great gift, but it will always lie beyond our ability to put into human words. This is so because the divine can never be captured by human thought. What is also very clear is that the response of the priest must not only be one of great gratitude, but also be an awareness of our call to a surpassing sanctity. It would be unconscionable for us priests to enter into this inestimable gift without availing ourselves of every means to live in holiness.

We respond not only by doing all we can to rid ourselves of grievous faults and sins, but also to attend increasingly to the smaller faults of our lives and to live our priestly vocation with a full integrity. We take care not to make the daily little decisions that can eventually lead us to the brink of major difficulties, being always aware how frail and prone to sin that we are. And we endeavor to live the essence of our priestly spirituality with a full heart.

Fortunately, this great sacrament of the Eucharist offers one final consolation. As in all sacraments, they make present what they signify; they bring to fruition what they celebrate. Just as the Eucharist calls the priest to holiness, it is also the most efficacious grace toward that end. The Eucharist itself is the priest's greatest means to true Christian holiness. Here, by the action of Christ, he is cleansed and raised up in the Spirit to the Father.

Thus, we go about our daily lives, although conscious of our human frailty, with an overriding trust in God. When we live our priestly vocations, day in and day out, the unseen action of grace slowly transforms us into what we were originally ordained to be. As the council fathers of Vatican II noted, "Priests who perform

> The priest offers the holy Sacrifice in persona Christi; this means more than offering "in the name of" or "in place of" Christ. In persona means in specific sacramental identification with "the eternal High Priest" who is the author and principal subject of this sacrifice of His, a sacrifice in which, in truth, nobody can take His place. . . . Awareness of this reality throws a certain light on the character and significance of the priest celebrant who, by confecting the holy Sacrifice and acting "in persona Christi," is sacramentally (and ineffably) brought into that most profound sacredness, and made part of it, spiritually linking with it in turn all those participating in the eucharistic assembly.
> —*Dominicae Cenae* 8

their duties sincerely and indefatigably in the Spirit of Christ arrive at holiness by this very fact" (*PO* 13).

As the priest strives toward holiness of life, he celebrates the Eucharist, which helps to make him holy.

The Eucharist itself is the priest's greatest means to true Christian holiness. Each day the sacrament of his configuration to Christ becomes more perfectly realized. Each day, the priest is increasingly transformed into the one whom he loves. And each day the priest ascends to the altar and pronounces the words that increasingly become his own, "This is my body. . . . This is my blood."

A JOURNAL ENTRY
Most Rev. Victor B. Galeone

The following is an entry from my journal in 1996 while I was the pastor of St. Agnes Church in Baltimore:

> Yesterday, after an emergency call at the nursing home, I was about to exit when I noticed a man in the hallway. He was sitting next to a woman in a wheelchair, tenderly holding her hands. Not a word was spoken. He just sat there, looking intently into her eyes. I walked over and engaged him in conversation:
>
> "Your wife, I take it?"
>
> "That's right, of forty-seven years."
>
> "Do you visit her often?"
>
> "Every single day. Haven't missed a day in four years, except for that blizzard last year."
>
> (During the exchange, his wife kept staring blankly into space.)
>
> "She's not saying anything."
>
> "That's right. Hasn't been able to for the last eighteen months—ever since her stroke. She has Alzheimer's too."

"Alzheimer's! Does she know who you are?"

"Not really. But that doesn't matter. I know who *she* is."

What an indictment against me, Lord Jesus! How often during my quiet time in your presence, I've kept one eye on the tabernacle and the other on my watch. Don't I deserve the same reprimand that your chosen three disciples received in the garden, "Could you not watch one hour with me?" Where is the love that should be animating my heart just as it did that of Saint Edith Stein when she remarked so lovingly, "He is truly *there*—and he is there for *me*!"

Had you been present on Calvary, with what devotion and tenderness you would have attended that great sacrifice! Enliven your faith, then, and consider that the same action is performed on the altar.
—St. Alphonsus Liguori[30]

Disconnected Eucharistic Memories
Rev. Stephen Wang

———

Sitting at the back of church as a teenager, refusing to kneel—because I had no faith and I was only there to please a friend—wondering what was going on, what made these people so quiet and attentive. . . .

Seeing the priest hold up the chalice and sensing with some dark, inarticulate knowledge, that there was a presence here that could not be found anywhere else; a presence that knew me. . . .

Visiting the cathedral one lunchtime, still an outsider, distracted by the peculiar mix of people at weekday Mass—workers on their lunch-break, tourists, the homeless, religious sisters, students, the elderly, parents and babies—people that should not have any business being together in the same place . . . yet they were. . . .

Standing up to profess my faith at my reception into full communion, walking up the aisle to receive my first Holy Communion, struck dumb and slightly scared by the enormity of what I understood, and even more by the enormity of what I didn't understand.
. . .

Holding the body of the Lord, now a priest, just after the consecration—thinking of Christ and Calvary and of the gift of Holy Communion—one part of me absorbed and caught up in the ritual, another part of me looking on, thinking "Who am I to be part of this mystery?". . .

Singing at the end of the Mass on retreat, an enormous crowd of young people and families; the spirit seemed to soar; a song that made me feel what I believe—that our worship is inseparable from the worship of heaven, the veil only paper thin; the whole Church gathered round the Lamb crying "Holy, holy, holy!" . . .

The Eucharist should be celebrated in joy, not only because Jesus instituted it in a climate of joy, but because, in it, Christ gives his own heavenly joy.
—Jean Galot, S.J.[31]

Preaching, just recently, at my tenth anniversary of priestly ordination; thanking God for the gift of faith and priesthood; and at the end, an unexpected joy, more than a mood, something silent, swift, spiritual; a reminder of the innocent wonder with which it all began . . .

A Surprising Gift of Belief
Rev. Kevin M. McDonough

———

The eucharistic Lord has always stood at the center of my priesthood. I love Masses large and small, festive and daily. Sunday worship in our parish is particularly powerful, and my own roles as presider and preacher still call forth from me—and give to me—enormous grace, energy, and satisfaction. But it was not until a year before my twenty-fifth anniversary that I was surprised by a particularly grace-filled gift. Having just lifted the cup of the newly consecrated blood of the Lord, and hearing the people sing the Mystery of Faith, I was moved in the very core of my being by this conviction: "I really believe this!"

Amazement and gratitude . . . should always fill the Church assembled for the celebration of the Eucharist. But in a special way it should fill the minister of the Eucharist.

—Ecclesia de Eucharistia 5

Let me be clear: I was not in any crisis of faith. Nor had I been wrestling with an intellectual doubt about the real presence. I was not "asking for a sign." And yet, God gave me a sign, perhaps a reminder. At the altar I am a presider and preacher, but first, I am a believer.

Since that moment of profound conviction, I have had echoes of the same experience. They come unbidden. In fact, I do not even seek them. It seems as if I could live from the clarity of that moment for the rest of my life.

Celebrating Mass continues to be a joy for me, not in spite of the many tasks involved, but right in the midst of them. I remember the soul for whom Mass is being offered, and watch for family members or friends in the congregation. The scriptures speak to me, and I try to pass on the little of their richness that I comprehend. Greeting the people at the sign of peace and after Mass is an encounter of blessing. But most of all, I am a believer. I am a believer.

For in the most blessed Eucharist is contained the entire spiritual wealth of the Church, namely Christ himself.
—Sacramentum Caritatis 16

GATHERING THE FRAGMENTS:
MAKING THE CONNECTIONS
Rev. Msgr. John Zenz

They saw a charcoal fire with fish on it and bread. Jesus
said to them, "Bring some of the fish you just caught." So
Simon and Peter went over and dragged the net ashore full
of one hundred-fifty-three large fish. Even though there
were so many, the net was not torn. Jesus said to them,
"Come have breakfast." . . . Jesus came over and took the
bread and gave it to them, and in like manner the fish.
—John 21:9–13

This article, a pastor's reflection on the Holy Eucharist, has been
a long time in coming. About three decades ago as a newly
ordained priest, meditating on John 21 and the Easter appearance
of Jesus to the disciples at the Sea of Tiberius, I had the inspiration
to write an article about the cycle of eucharistic ministry: *receiving*
blessings, *offering* them back to the Lord, and then *receiving* them
again in a new, transformed way. Then the cycle begins once more.
The eucharistic process never ends. In fact, it becomes deeper and
richer as we share more consciously in Christ's eternal action of
receiving all and returning all to the Father.

We see the three moments of this cycle quite clearly in John 21.
Totally frustrated by their failure to catch any fish all night long, the
disciples received the surprising gift of a miraculous catch. Then the
Lord asked them to hand over their newfound treasure. They did so
without hesitation for they knew the fish were never theirs in the

107

first place. Having given him the fish, they received them back as a tasty breakfast, a gift transformed. Herein rests a message for us: as we receive and return all good gifts to the Lord—including our very selves, all our hopes and dreams, fears and pains—we experience a new consecration of our gifts and ourselves. These are indeed the three "moments" of the Eucharist: the offering of bread and wine and ourselves; the acceptance and consecration of our gifts; and then a new deeper communion with the Lord and each other.

For a variety of reasons, I never got around to writing the article. Now, in the providence of God, insights from thirty years ago have been seasoned by the joys and sorrows of ministry in diverse settings. Like the Eucharist itself, I have been changed. Hopefully these reflections will be a testament to the work of God's grace through me and the people I have been privileged to serve.

Had this article been written in 1980, I would have titled it, "Making the Connections." Already as a young priest, I realized that our daily service involves helping our people to make the connections between their life experiences and the powerful, but often hidden, presence of the Lord in his word and sacrament.

A Pastor's Perspective

I must start with a confession. When Msgr. Rossetti invited me to contribute to this collection on a priestly spirituality of the Eucharist, he asked that I write specifically as a *pastor*. I have served as a priest for three decades, but technically speaking, I have been a pastor for only a few months. But, thanks to God's goodness, I have always had the heart of a pastor and was able to maintain an ongoing connection with the same parish community for a quarter century.

I have also enjoyed the opportunity of being an episcopal vicar for three years, rotating from parish to parish within my geographic jurisdiction, presiding at Confirmations, parish anniversaries, and installations of pastors. While it is energizing to experience different communities, being with the same congregation Sunday after Sunday is truly more consoling. However, being a pastor also brings many immediate responsibilities and expectations. A pastor faces the challenge of being fresh day after day, year after year. Being an occasional visitor, you can be the charming "stranger in paradise," but as a pastor bonded with a permanent community, the needs of the people call you to ever deeper levels of the Spirit. Immersed in the lives of my parishioners, I am at once the more deeply immersed in Christ.

As an episcopal vicar, time and again, I have heard parishioners say that one of the main criteria that motivated them to choose a certain parish had to do with the quality of the liturgy and the way the priest celebrated it. They could accept disappointing homilies and poor administrative skills if their pastor was truly prayerful in the way he was present to them and to the Lord at the altar.

From my various ministerial experiences, it seems to me that every priest, especially a pastor, has the challenge of making the connections, remembering and matching the many gifts and diverse needs of his staff and parishioners. How does he do it? By skillful organization? Through inspiring preaching? No, the priest cannot do it on his own; Christ

> In addition, the nature of the ministerial priesthood also puts into its proper light another reality, which must indeed be highly regarded, namely, the royal priesthood of the faithful, whose spiritual sacrifice is brought to completeness through the ministry of the Bishop and the priests in union with the sacrifice of Christ, the one and only Mediator. For the celebration of the Eucharist is an action of the whole Church.
> —General Instruction on the Roman Missal 5

does it *through* him at the altar. The priest makes the connections primarily in and through the celebration of Christ's Eucharist, "the source and summit" of our lives, the sacrifice and nourishment that calls our Church into being.

Making the connections refers to our priestly service of being a "living memory" of and for the community. We teach the tradition of faith and interpret the scriptures for ourselves and our people. Above all, we embody for our parishioners their connection to the wider Church with its long history and rich diversity as we celebrate the Holy Eucharist, the memorial sacrifice that shapes our lives, the backdrop against which we measure all the stories of our lives.

As priests, in the celebration of the Holy Eucharist, we help our communities "re-member" our identity and our mission. Our parishioners also challenge *us* to stretch our own memories. "Re-membering" is a dynamic process that not only recalls and integrates past events into the present; we also remember the *future*. In fact, every eucharistic celebration truly points toward the future banquet of the Kingdom and challenges us to remember the reason for our hope. "Making the connections" challenges us to live in three "time zones"—past, present, and future—all at the same time, finding the gifts of God hidden at every moment of the journey.

Gathering the Fragments

With the blessing of thirty years of priestly service, I see that "making the connections" could also be phrased, "gathering the fragments." A pastor not only brings the past and future to bear in the present moment, he also seeks to assure his people that *nothing* of the past is outside the realm of grace and that whatever pain the uncertain future holds, it too is capable of becoming something beautiful for God. Nothing and no one is to be lost or forgotten. Like Jesus, the Good Shepherd, a pastor seeks to draw into the family of faith all those who might otherwise be overlooked or forgotten.

Over the years I have come to see how John 21 connects with the earlier eucharistic miracle of John 6, the multiplication of the loaves and fishes in the desert. Like the scene of the risen Lord at the seashore, John 6 also speaks of connecting and gathering. At the end of the story of multiplication of the loaves and fishes, Jesus directed his disciples to "gather up the fragments so that nothing will go to waste."

By his own word and example, Christ teaches that a vital part of every Eucharist includes "gathering the fragments," that is, the incomplete and unfulfilled joys and dreams of our people and ourselves. Ultimately, it is the Lord who does the gathering. It is our privilege to be his instruments, helping our people appreciate the sustaining presence of God, which encompasses us and holds us together, especially in times of apparent loss and struggle.

SEEING JESUS

In my pastoral ministry I daily rejoice in the poetic wisdom of Gerard Manley Hopkins' line, "Christ plays in ten thousand places, lovely in eyes and limbs not his—to the Father through the features of men's faces." In the Church where I serve, people surround me on all sides and I have learned to let the Christ in them "speak" to me even as I strive to be the Lord's instrument for them. The crying baby and fidgety child are no

> Though they differ from one another in essence and not only in degree, the common priesthood of the faithful and the ministerial or hierarchical priesthood are nonetheless interrelated: each of them in its own special way is a participation in the one priesthood of Christ. The ministerial priest, by the sacred power he enjoys, teaches and rules the priestly people; acting in the person of Christ, he makes present the eucharistic sacrifice, and offers it to God in the name of all the people. But the faithful, in virtue of their royal priesthood, join in the offering of the Eucharist. They likewise exercise that priesthood in receiving the sacraments, in prayer and thanksgiving, in the witness of a holy life, and by self-denial and active charity.
> —*Lumen Gentium* 10

longer nuisances to be tolerated, but sharers with me in Christ's prayer of praise and thanks.

As a pastor celebrating the Eucharist, I cannot help but notice the many little details—the smile, frown, or puzzled look on someone's face, the sleeping child resting on mom or dad's shoulder, the awkward slump of someone struggling with arthritis, the ushers chattering at the doorways, the father of a family arriving late (having dropped off everyone else) and looking for the rest of his clan, a radiant newly married couple, a grieving widow or widower. As my eyes connect with this or that parishioner, we both recall a meeting to be scheduled, a phone call yet to be returned, the unresolved pain of disagreement from a recent parish council meeting. The list goes on and on; you know it as well as I. I struggle to see and *not* to see, to see and to "let go," to recognize things and people who are "out of sorts," but yet not to worry about an immediate solution. Fragments must be noticed and respected before they can ever be gathered.

As I reflect on the challenge of truly seeing my parishioners with the eyes of Christ, I cannot help but recall the story of a contemporary English Redemptorist priest who is both deaf and blind. Somehow, he faithfully ministers to people of all backgrounds. How blessed we are to be able to *see* our parishioners!

Perhaps a personal example can further illustrate "gathering the fragments" as a means for being changed and renewed. Taking Viaticum to a lawyer from our parish, near death from stomach cancer, I arrived to find him still alert and able to speak, but he could no longer swallow. Since he could not receive communion, he said, "Give Nancy the host. I'll receive my communion through her. After all, that's what we have been doing as husband and wife for forty years now." Communion together in Christ comes as we let go of our agendas and let the Lord gather the fragments of our lives. As we do so, our sacrifices and struggles fade in significance and we begin to realize we are truly sharing in his sacrifice.

BEING EMPTY FOR JESUS TO SPEAK AND ACT

To be able to "gather the fragments," we need to be in a state of emptiness, a mode of absolute receptivity to all that will be given, to all that will happen. That means setting aside worries about meeting people's expectations and refusing to dwell on present frustrations or past disappointments. It means taking time for some quiet before, and after, the celebration of the Eucharist. In my own experience as a celebrant, I often have to drive to and from various places. I try to use that time for quiet contemplation, praying for openness to all the people I will meet, and then on the way home, thanking God for having used me. The silence and emptiness before and after the Eucharist makes a great difference in the spiritual fruitfulness of this great sacrament for me personally.

Years ago, I remember working with a veteran pastor who about an hour before Mass used to say that he was going to his room to "gather his thoughts" before he went over to celebrate Sunday Eucharist. His expression "gather my thoughts" catches something of the dynamism of being a celebrant of the Eucharist. The pause that we take after saying, "Let us pray," just before we offer the collect or opening prayer, the Church's prayer which draws together all our disparate wants and needs, fears and hopes, desires and dreams. Are we not trying to say: "Let us be gathered so that we can pray," or, "Let us be emptied of our own agendas so that Christ can pray in us and through us to the glory of the Father." We celebrate the Eucharist most prayerfully when we are physically, and spiritually, a bit hungry. Like the disciples at the shore of Tiberias, a hidden energy seems to rise out of our own spiritual emptiness, darkness, and weakness.

I recall one Christmas Eve years ago. There was a terrible division among the staff, and the pastor was ill. Although quite young in the ministry, I was alone and in charge. I discovered accidentally that "they" were having their own Christmas party—on our premises and without having even invited me! At first I was flushed with anger and brooded, considering ways to "get even." But then I prayed for the grace to let go and be empty for the several Masses

I would be celebrating that evening. It worked. I had one of the holiest and most spiritually energizing Christmases ever.

We ourselves will be all the more nourished, as we lose ourselves in the prayers of the Eucharist and let the "cycle" of the eucharistic process run its course through us. Over the years I have come to appreciate more and more the importance of reciting, or singing, the words of the Eucharistic Prayer slowly and deliberately, emphasizing phrases that are particularly connected with the season or the readings. We do not need to be especially creative, but just let the words speak for themselves.

Our former ordinary, Cardinal John Dearden, had as his episcopal motto *Servio in Evangelio*, a phrase from the first chapter of St. Paul's letter to the Romans, *"I serve in the gospel."* Implicit in the motto was the confession that he was *under* the gospel and sought to conform himself to it, not vice-versa. The same struggle is true for us as celebrants. We are called to pray the words of the Eucharist just as the Church has given them. After all, it is the prayer of the *Church*. But we need to do it with fresh enthusiasm each time. As priests, like our people and with our people, we must enter into *Christ's* prayer and *Christ's* action.

> The Church which is the Body of Christ participates in the offering of her Head. With him, she herself is offered whole and entire. She unites herself to his intercession with the Father for all men. In the Eucharist the sacrifice of Christ becomes also the sacrifice of the members of his Body. The lives of the faithful, their praise, sufferings, prayer, and work, are united with those of Christ and with his total offering, and so acquire a new value.
> —*Catechism of the Catholic Church* 1368

A friend of mine used to jog with me on Monday mornings and would often critique my Sunday homily and eucharistic celebration. More than once, his observation was, "Too much John, not enough Jesus." Being empty of self in every way possible makes a critical difference for our people to be able to see Jesus. We also need to be empty for our own sake so that we will truly be touched and changed by the celebration of the Lord's dying and rising. I keep reminding myself that liturgy is the work of the Lord, a *public* work. Paradoxically, I am a more powerful and effective instrument of Christ to the extent that my own emotions and preferences do not come into play. Simply put, I try to get out of the Lord's way so that Christ, and Christ alone, might be priest *for* me and *through* me. I also try to remember that the priestly people of God are also Christ to me for they model the cycle and moments of the holy Eucharist in their own lives.

CHANGED AND CHANGING

We call ourselves "presiders" and so we are, but sometimes we take the word too literally. Ultimately, it is the Lord who presides; we are his representatives. When I focus too much on my own responsibilities or liturgical preferences, I can easily get caught up in issues of pride, worried about doing everything perfectly. When I remind myself that I am praying *with* and *for* the community, then I remember I am part of a larger drama. Crying babies and the inevitable interruptions and frustrations are not really obstacles but blessings, part of the surprising beauty of what we do *with* God and *for* God. Like the disciples who had caught nothing all night long, the Lord gives us nourishment precisely in the brokenness of our struggles and helps us gather the fragments, all that

> Thus the Eucharistic Action is the very heartbeat of the congregation of the faithful over which the priest presides. So priests must instruct them to offer to God the Father the divine Victim in the sacrifice of the Mass, and to join to it the offering of their own lives.
> —*Presbyterorum Ordinis* 5

which is unresolved in our own hearts. Only then are we ready to help our people gather all their brokenness as well, helping them believe that the Lord truly wants *nothing* of their experiences ever to be lost, wasted, or forgotten. All is valuable. All is worthy of being offered. All can be healed, consecrated, transformed and reserved. Just when we "hit the wall," the Lord surprises us and leads us to discover new depths and new potential, within us and among us.

The Eucharist celebrates *change*—the transubstantiation of the bread and wine into the body and blood of the Lord, and the transformation of all who share these gifts. After the eucharistic celebration, we should be different than before we started. Having shared communion with my parishioners, I cannot help but find new joy and peace as I reflect on their daily generous sacrifices of love. By the time Mass ends, the full impact of what we have been doing usually hits me: we have been uniting our sacrifices to those of Christ, confident that in some mysterious way, everything and everyone is sacred.

I am reminded of an insight from a Trappist monk of Gethsemani to the effect that Benedictine spirituality is about "being good with other people's goodness." These words are an excellent commentary on the way a pastor celebrates the Eucharist and fulfills all his ministry—noticing, rejoicing, and affirming all the gifts of his people and then joining them in thanking God, the giver of every blessing. Like the disciples on the seashore in John 21, sometimes it takes a while for our vision to adjust. Then, our hearts recognize the risen Lord at work in the way our parishioners are growing in holiness through their own daily embrace of the cross.

A Meal Unfinished

About ten years ago, walking back to our chancery from the nearby parking garage, I encountered a beggar—a frequent occurrence in that depressed part of the city. It was surprising that he was there alone in the middle of the afternoon; most of the beggars came at the beginning or end of the workday. His was a face I had never seen before. Holding out a handful of coins, he asked for thirty-three cents so that he would have enough money to buy a ninety-nine-cent fish sandwich as advertised on the billboard in front of the "greasy spoon" next door to the chancery.

I reached into my pocket and handed him all the change I had, considerably more than the specific amount requested. He took offense saying he wasn't looking for charity! I apologized, laughed, and said, "Enjoy your lunch," and proceeded to walk briskly toward the safety of the chancery doorway just a few yards away. But he called to me, "Come back here, Father." And so I returned, presuming he wanted more money.

Instead he asked: "Have *you* had lunch?" I hesitated, thinking if I said yes perhaps he'd complain I was just giving him "fragments," my coins, for a lousy fish sandwich while I (presumably) had eaten something more healthy and more substantial. So I said, "No, I have not had much of a lunch" (technically true—a salad without protein at a luncheon with the Christ Child ladies). Then he really got me with his next line,

> The Eucharist includes, more precisely, the invitation to offer all that in our lives that is sorrowful or painful, with our gaze fixed on the heroic offering of Calvary. Painful as our sufferings may be, we should "intend" not only our sufferings properly so called, but also our anguish, our sometimes vexing concerns, our moral situations with all of the interior dramas that explode outwardly or that remain concealed, our tensions of every kind in our relationships with others. All that is experienced in our daily round deserves to be carried as an offering to the Eucharist, in order to receive there a higher dignity through an assimilation to the redemptive suffering of Christ.
> —*The Eucharist, Gift of Divine Life*[32]

"Since we *both* are buying the fish sandwich would you like to have lunch with me? Maybe we could share it."

Pausing, I tried to picture his (presumably) dirty hands breaking the greasy fish sandwich in two. I thought if I sit down with him where might this go? He would "know" me and might expect things from me . . . a relationship, a friendship . . . with a beggar?! I politely declined, claiming I had a meeting and again headed quickly for the chancery doorway. He called me back yet again and when I arrived exasperated, he asked: "Father would you have lunch with me *another* day?"

Embarrassed, I looked him in the eyes for the first time. I'd never seen such beautiful deep brown eyes . . . and a handsome face. I suddenly realized I was speaking with an angel, maybe the Lord himself. What could I do now, though? I had painted myself into a corner and I was too proud to change my mind. All I could do was stammer, "Yes, of course. Another day."

With that I darted into the chancery. A minute later I rethought things and went back out on the street but he was gone. Nor was he to be found in the sandwich shop. He had vanished— but *without* the "breaking of the bread." I realized then that I had missed a gift. I have often thought of the passage from Revelation 3:20: "Behold, I stand at the door and knock." In the years since I've been watching for that man but to this day he has never reappeared. For my part, I keep looking. This experience has changed how I look at all beggars. Now I see *myself* as a beggar *with* them, looking for Christ.

Every Eucharist is an unfinished meal. In every Eucharist we proclaim the powerful presence of Christ hidden in broken fragments gathered with love and compassion. Somehow the cycle of gift received and given back is never finished this side of heaven. There is always someone, somewhere who is hungry and needing to break bread.

THE CYCLE CONTINUES

Perhaps the best way to end these reflections on the cycle of the Holy Eucharist is by way of an analogy, a story from my childhood that partially describes the process of receiving well, giving back, and receiving anew in a transformed way. When I was young, I had a paper route. I could afford to buy small presents for my mother's birthday, Mother's Day, etc. Other than occasional babysitting, my three sisters had no outside income, and therefore had to be more creative when it came to gift-giving. They used to take pieces from my mother's jewelry box, wrap them and present them as if they were a brand new purchase. My mother knowingly but graciously opened their gifts remarking, "Oh, I think I have a necklace that will match these earrings."

Years later, when all of us were together with Mom, jokingly, I asked if she had not thought my sisters cheap since they simply recycled her jewelry instead of buying her something brand new. Mom smiled and said that it did not bother her in the least. She explained that she felt twice blessed for the jewelry; the gift originally from my Father was now all the more beautiful because it had the fingerprints of her daughters.

Here is the cycle of the Holy Eucharist and the ministry of a pastor. Like the disciples at the shore of Tiberias, we often "hit the wall." We find ourselves lacking in resources, strength, energy, and vision. But just as we confess our limits, God always surprises us with new gifts. As he challenged Abraham to be ready to sacrifice his beloved Isaac, God is always asking us to be willing to hand to him all that we have, all that we are, all that we had hoped to become, our failures and disappointments, our apparent successes, discoveries, and insights. Every blessing must be returned. Again and again, he invites us to live in a state of Advent emptiness and hopefulness. As we trust him, we suddenly discover our nets are surprisingly full. Even better, we realize the Lord is right there on the shore waiting to share breakfast with us.

ENTERING THE PASCHAL MYSTERY
Rev. Daniel P. Coughlin

Shortly after my ordination, Pope Paul VI called the liturgy "our school of spirituality." While I had always understood the centrality of the Eucharist to our spirituality, his use of this phrase led me to reflect on the quality of my preaching. How could I preach in a way that helped the faithful to truly appreciate the liturgy as "our school of spirituality"?

This was a learning process for me. About that time I remember attending a conference on racial tensions, where I admitted to brother priests that I often preached in a way that I hoped would make people feel good and return the following week. This was a long way from preaching and celebrating the liturgy as "our school of spirituality." So I began to preach more about the paschal mystery. But I see now that I was simply imposing the paschal paradigm of death and resurrection of Christ onto contemporary happenings. I wanted to help people live the ups and downs of life. But deep down, I knew I had oversimplified the paschal nature of Eucharist.

I finally came to appreciate the lived reality of the paschal mystery while on sabbatical with the Missionaries of Charity in Calcutta. There I heard the Word offering consolation to hopelessly poor people. There I experienced the Eucharist as people laying down their lives with the dying in the street. In their surrender simply to be one with their brothers and sisters, Christ was revealed to me as living and active in them.

Now I appreciate in a whole new way that the paschal mystery is not something that exists outside the baptized, but within and among us. Christ moves and acts in the people of God. Now I find such delight in preaching the paschal mystery, uncovering how Christ is transforming us, moving in us, and bringing us into the fullness of his life. The Eucharist celebrates the union of Christ and his Church. Preaching helps people understand that Christ's redemptive act is not simply histori-cal, but is taking place in and through them, here and now. They are the body of Christ, and the Father takes great delight in them. So, we offer praise and thanks.

Given the importance of the word of God, the quality of homilies needs to be improved.
—Sacramentum Caritatis 46

AT MASS WITH PADRE PIO
Rev. Msgr. Paul A. Lenz

In 1964, Bishop J. Carroll McCormick, the bishop of my diocese of Altoona-Johnstown, invited me to accompany him to Rome for the final session of the Vatican Council. While in Rome, the bishop suggested that I take a few days and visit the monastery in southern Italy where Padre Pio lived.

When I arrived at 2:00 a.m., I found a very long line of people waiting for the doors of the church to open. I got in line and stood with the crowd. At about 4:00 a.m., a Capuchin friar in brown habit came along and, seeing me in a black suit and collar, asked if I was a priest. Replying yes, he invited me to follow him to the church where we entered by a side door. I was ushered into the first pew in front of the altar.

Padre Pio arrived at the altar at 5:00 a.m. and stood with a long, prayerful pause, not moving, almost like being in a trance. He began Mass and from that moment as I watched him, I, too, felt seized and transported by grace. I was completely absorbed in the Mass. The look on Padre Pio's face seemed to be totally different in appearance from when he walked to the altar. If it is possible to say that one gets more devout, Padre Pio appeared to be in a complete ecstasy. The Mass proceeded slowly, taking over two hours. I remember Padre Pio paused many times and seemed totally absorbed in the prayers of the Mass. I could not take my eyes off him. When he came to recite the prayers of the consecration, there was another definite change in his face. I do not think I will ever

123

forget that change. When he received the body and blood of Christ, I sensed that he was in total union with Jesus.

After the Mass, the priests were invited into the sacristy to greet Padre Pio. We were able to take his hand, and he had a word or two in Italian and a smile for each. I remember saying, "Please, Padre Pio, your blessing."

Still years later, when he comes to mind, I continue to have the same intense feeling of awe and grace as the day I attended the Mass and personally held the hand of Padre Pio.

At every celebration of the Eucharist, we are spiritually brought back to the paschal Triduum.
—Ecclesia de Eucharistia 3

The Luckiest People on Earth

Rev. Brendan Daly

A woman I know, brought up a Catholic, went to a Catholic boarding school, and eventually gave up practicing her faith. She married and had three children who were not baptized. When the children were teenagers, she went to the Catholic funeral of a friend. She sat down in the back of the church. When it came time for communion, she watched the people going up to receive the Eucharist. She thought to herself, "If those people receiving communion are receiving the Son of God, they must be the luckiest people on earth." Reflecting on this led her to come back to the practice of her faith.

The Eucharist is . . . a glòrious ray of the heavenly Jerusalem which pierces the clouds of our history and lights up our journey.
—Ecclesia de Eucharistia *19*

THE EUCHARIST—HEART OF THE PRIEST'S LIFE
Rev. Gabriel B. O'Donnell, O.P.

———

The Eucharist has always been the center of my life. Before entering religious life, I attended daily Mass. This was not universal among teens in the 1950s, but neither was it unusual. Visits to the Blessed Sacrament in quiet and darkened churches were common in my generation. We individually made the Stations of the Cross and said the Rosary in such settings. Or we simply visited with Our Lord present in the reserved sacrament.

Struggles with parents and peers, and worries about poor grades and the dangers of unchastity, were typical Catholic teen concerns that were brought to Christ in the Eucharist. Benediction of the Blessed Sacrament was for many a high point in our devotional life, but that was the only form of exposition we knew. I later encountered long periods of exposition in the chapel of the nearby monastery of Dominican cloistered nuns. Exposition was "perpetual" there, as was the nuns' prayer of the Rosary.

Today, having navigated the monumental changes following the Second Vatican Council and having weathered the ecclesial crises of the second half of the last century, it is clear that the first decade of the twenty-first century is witnessing a new brand of young Catholics. Searching for stability and continuity with the past, fervent young men and women today are decidedly more eucharistic in their attachment to exposition of the Blessed

Sacrament, holy hours, and new forms of eucharistic devotion. All this is in addition to attendance at daily Mass.

The promise of the New Evangelization and the religious and priests shaped by it brings new hope for the future. The inroads into Catholic life and culture made by twentieth century secularism are being challenged by the rising generation's insistence that it is only within the tradition of sound theological reflection and authentic Christian spirituality that we will find our way into the future. What may appear to older Catholics like a return to the past, a nostalgic return to the Church of the 1950s, is for those who understand the New Evangelization, a path to the future. It is a future that promises a renewal of faith and a spirit of enthusiasm for the gospel.

The promise of the New Evangelization and the religious and priests shaped by it brings new hope for the future.

THE REAL PRESENCE

Because it was the bedrock of the faith of our parents, few Catholics of my era questioned the notion of the true presence of Christ in the eucharistic species. We were schooled in the catechism definitions, knew how to explain transubstantiation, and followed our parents, teachers, and priests in reverencing the sacred host and all things related to the Holy Sacrifice of the Mass.

The first time I heard the phrase "body and blood, soul and divinity" referring to the mode of Christ's eucharistic presence, I was preparing for First Communion. I had no idea what it really meant, but I knew that when the priest placed the host on my tongue I would meet Jesus Christ in a most remarkable and intimate way because he was somehow in the host. I was not disappointed.

I have no memories of religious emotion or spiritual transports, but from that day until this, a certain clarity of mind has been mine. On that day, it became clear that attaining heaven was the most critical issue in life. It seemed to me then, as now, that belonging to God was the most remarkable thing possible for a human life. Not many days have passed since then when I have not pondered these two realities, and they have shaped all of my life decisions. My awareness of a religious vocation began on that day.

I often puzzled over that phrase, so carefully memorized and repeated, "body and blood, soul and divinity," and it was only years later, in preparation for the priesthood, that its meaning became clear. As a child, even without fully comprehending, I clung to those words, knowing that they contained a mystery that was vital to my faith.

The Eucharist is the center of the Christian life precisely because it brings God to us.

It is often the case that children hold onto things learned early in life, although little understood. In time, meanings unfold. Life gradually reveals itself to us and we must learn to wait in expectation and patience. Often the religious truths memorized in formal and foreign sounding phrases during early religious formation later come alive with a clarity and vitality that makes possible a deeper faith commitment. What is first known only through the intuition of faith is more clearly articulated with mature thinking and a more precise vocabulary. Faith matures.

The Eucharist is the center of the Christian life precisely because it brings God to us. The bread of God is Jesus who, in giving himself to us as "food for truth," brings the Father to us and brings us to the Father. In the Eucharist he "gives us the totality of his life and reveals the ultimate origin of . . . love" (*S Car* 7). Since the transformation of the bread and wine into his body and blood is accomplished through the action of the Holy Spirit, the Eucharist is the sacrament of Trinitarian love in a unique way.

The Priest as Sacrament

The priest, ordained precisely to be a eucharistic person, is, of necessity, at the heart of the Church and most himself when he stands at the altar of Christ. His identity, as a priest, flows from the words of consecration, "This is my body. . . . This is my blood." Uniquely among the People of God, St. Paul's words are proper to the priest, "For me to live is Christ." At the Last Supper, our Lord revealed his intended way to continually become present in our midst. It is through the transformation of bread and wine into his body and blood at the hands of the priest. "Do this in remembrance of me."

We can only conclude that a priestly spirituality is always, fundamentally, a eucharistic spirituality. The often expressed desire for a more developed spirituality of the priesthood, particularly for diocesan priests, must always find its foundation and fulfillment in the Eucharist. It is in the Mass that the priest will find his true identity and the means to become more perfectly conformed to Christ the High Priest who is also the immaculate Lamb of Sacrifice and the Shepherd of Souls.

> The intention of ensuring the daily celebration of the Eucharist in the Church reveals a special characteristic of the eucharistic heart of Jesus: the desire to give himself to the maximum in order to fulfil to the maximum the spiritual needs of the human race. . . . In giving his Son, the Father wanted to give everything. The Son, in giving himself as daily food, highlights the Father's gift, the summit of divine generosity.
> —Jean Galot[33]

As a consequence, the priest becomes a living sacramental sign of the presence of Jesus Christ in our midst, in our world. This is a heavy office to bear because the priest is held to a higher standard than the ordinary Christian. The Catholic faithful have expectations regarding the depth of the priest's interior life and the example of his exterior behavior. Accepting his human frailty and imperfections, they nonetheless look for spiritual inspiration and moral guidance from their priests. A priest must live close to the Eucharist if he is to fulfill the expectations of the Church and the people in his pastoral ministry.

Pope Benedict has affirmed that priests of the Latin rite are called to celibacy precisely because they must act *in persona Christi capitis*. It is fitting that the priest should follow the example of the Lord himself who "lived his mission even to the sacrifice of the cross in the state of virginity" (*S Car* 24). It is this high ideal of holiness and perfection that underlies the tradition of clerical celibacy. The call to carry heavy burdens, his own and those of his people, is an integral part of the spirituality of the priesthood. We are quick to promise young men considering the priesthood the support and consolation that comes from caring for God's people. Less emphasized is the challenge of being a sacrament of Christ's presence in the world, a challenge that requires spiritual as well as human maturity. The Eucharist is the primary source from which this strength, wisdom, and pastoral charity comes. The work of the priest is, before all else, sacramental and spiritual.

The call to carry heavy burdens, his own and those of his people, is an integral part of the spirituality of the priesthood.

SACRAMENTAL SIGNS

A sacrament, in simple terms, is a sign. It is always a sign of our salvation. Words and actions, chosen by Christ, make present his saving work through the power of the Holy Spirit. In this sense, sacraments are signs come down from heaven, and each of them has a reality to communicate, something necessary for our salvation and sanctification. The Angelic Doctor teaches that in every sacrament there are three things to be considered: the *cause* of our sanctification, which is Christ's passion, death and resurrection, that is, the paschal mystery; the *essence* of our sanctification, which is grace and virtue; and the *goal* of our sanctification, which is eternal life (*Summa* III, 60.3). In a manner reminiscent of the memorial acclamation at Mass, St. Thomas sees in each sacrament the summation of past, present, and future.

In the sacraments, God, in Christ, acts. He acts for our salvation and sanctification. The Eucharist contains the incarnate second person of the Blessed Trinity, body and blood, soul and divinity. Jesus Christ, true God and true man, comes to us under the appearances of bread and wine. What begets wonder, hesitation and holy fear in the child, begets reverence, gratitude and deep spiritual hunger in the mature man.

Just as I need to eat, I need the daily celebration of the Eucharist.

The question of *daily* celebration of Mass, sometimes debated among priests, has always puzzled me. When I have had to forego saying Mass because of sickness or travel, I have missed it. Even attending Mass and receiving Holy Communion is not the same, because it is not the full expression of who I am as a eucharistic man, as a priest. As truly as missing a meal does not go unnoticed, the failure to celebrate daily Mass creates a spiritual hunger within. Just as I need to eat, I need the daily celebration of the Eucharist. Christ, in the Eucharist, becomes the "food of truth," and our companion on the journey of life. The more intimately one enters into this mystery, the more one feeds off the bread come down from heaven (cf Jn 6:32–33).

The Eucharist, as the sacrament to which the other sacraments lead and from which they flow, makes present past events that both transform the present and prepare us for the future. The priest, as celebrant of the Mass, has the responsibility of keeping these aspects clear and alive in the manner and style of his liturgical leadership. Nowhere is this more the case than in the Eucharist. The cult of the personality must disappear when one enters the sanctuary, and the priest must allow himself to be the sacrament of Christ the victim and the priest. The Eucharist requires of the priest a degree of humility that calls forth a virtuous life and presumes a life of daily prayer. A priestly, eucharistic spirituality rests on the basis that the grace of the Eucharist will become the transformative principle on the priest's life and person.

The celebration of daily Mass is an important part of a true priestly spirituality. There the priest meets Christ the High Priest and receives from him what is needed for a true life of union with God and a true life of pastoral service devoid of ego and arrogance. The commitment to daily celebration of Mass is less the observance of some rule of the spiritual life and more an act of faith in the truth of Christ's promise that anyone who eats his flesh and drinks his blood will have life everlasting. Daily Mass is the priest's path into eternity.

EUCHARISTIC COMMUNION

The eucharistic communion that occurs when I, in my weak and sinful humanity, encounter Jesus Christ in his sacred humanity, is a communion with him, body and blood, soul and divinity. It is the meeting of human natures that becomes the instrument of the encounter between me and the second person of the Blessed

> By the power of the sacrament of orders, and in the image of Christ the eternal High Priest, they are consecrated to preach the gospel, shepherd the faithful, and celebrate divine worship as true priests of the New Testament. Partakers of the function of Christ the sole Mediator on their level of ministry, they announce the divine word to all. They exercise this sacred function of Christ most of all in the Eucharistic liturgy or synaxis. There, acting in the person of Christ, and proclaiming His mystery, they join the offering of the faithful to the sacrifice of their Head. Until the coming of the Lord, they re-present and apply in the Sacrifice of the Mass the one sacrifice of the New Testament, namely the sacrifice of Christ offering himself once and for all to his Father as a spotless victim.
> —*Lumen Gentium* 28

Trinity. In the Eucharist there is a meeting of the divine and the human. There is a communion. The dynamic inferred in the word "communion" is more than simple reception on the part of the communicant. Christ comes in his humanity and divinity. We who receive him now "touch" the divine. However, speaking of Jesus coming to me and striving to be focused on him at the moment of communion, to encounter him in intimacy and love is but one aspect of the reality of eucharistic communion.

The grace of the Eucharist will become the transformative principle on the priest's life and person.

I meet Christ in eucharistic communion because he himself has willed to come to me in his sacred humanity so that I may begin to know him in his divine nature. He wills that I should know him as he is. He is the only begotten of the Father. He is in the Father and the Father is in him. He wills that I should know him in the love that goes between him and the Father, that love which is the Holy Spirit. *We might speak more properly of Christ, in his sacred humanity, receiving us in the Eucharist into the communion of his divine life of Trinitarian love.*

This has profound implications for a true eucharistic spirituality. For in the Eucharist, Jesus Christ is made present as he is now, seated at the right hand of the Father, directing the Holy Spirit to continue his work of salvation and transformation begun during his human life on earth. That he should continue to give himself to us in his own body and blood, through the instrument of his sacred humanity, suggests the goodness and importance of all things human, most especially those joined to him in Baptism. As his sacred humanity becomes the sacramental instrument of our sanctification, so our humanity is now an instrument for our progressive transformation into the image of God. Marred by sin and our resistance to grace, that image must be restored and brought to perfection in the Eucharist.

An authentic eucharistic spirituality must always honor the innate goodness of human nature. It must recognize that Christ, in assuming his own human nature, has now elevated all human nature. Our humanity is as much our way to heaven as his way to earth. He is the bread that comes down from heaven so that we, in our eating and drinking, may find our way to heaven itself. The Eucharist sanctifies us through the conformity of our humanity to his, and in that conformity he joins us to his divine life of Trinitarian love and communion.

In the study of theology we commonly say that in the face of all that we know about God we must admit that it is but a fraction of what we do not know about God. In a true eucharistic spirituality, we must acknowledge that whatever we experience in eucharistic communion, no matter how sublime, even mystical, it is less than the reality of what God is doing in the depths of our humanity, in our souls, when we partake of the Eucharist. The sacraments sanctify and transform according to God's plan for each of us.

THE MASS IS A SACRIFICE

The notion of the sacrificial character of the Mass has been muted in ordinary Catholic

Unfortunately, alongside these lights, there are also shadows. In some places the practice of Eucharistic adoration has been almost completely abandoned. In various parts of the Church, abuses have occurred, leading to confusion with regard to sound faith and Catholic doctrine concerning this wonderful sacrament. At times one encounters an extremely reductive understanding of the Eucharistic mystery. Stripped of its sacrificial meaning, it is celebrated as if it were simply a fraternal banquet. Furthermore, the necessity of the ministerial priesthood, grounded in apostolic succession, is at times obscured. . . . How can we not express profound grief at all this? The Eucharist is too great a gift to tolerate ambiguity and depreciation.
—*Ecclesia de Eucharistia* 10

teaching in the last few decades. Without clarity on this point, there is no true theology of the Eucharist. It is precisely in the laying down of his life, the giving of his body and blood for our salvation, that Jesus Christ has atoned for our sins and made possible our sharing in his life of communion with the Father and the Holy Spirit. In every Mass, Christ's sacrifice of himself is made present again, and the effects of that sacrifice are brought to us by the action of the Spirit. Ritually symbolized by the separate consecrations of the bread and the wine, the sacrifice of Calvary is made present again in every Mass, "in an unbloody manner," to quote the catechism of my youth.

The suffering and struggles of the priest have salvific purpose.

In every Mass, it is his body that is offered to the Father; it is his blood that is offered to the Father. The reality of Christ's passion and death become sacramentally present on the altar at every Mass. Is it any wonder that so many saints warn the priest about the need to be well prepared for the Eucharist by a life of prayer and virtue? The renewed popularity of the phrase "the Holy Sacrifice of the Mass" in our time is evidence of a hunger among younger Catholics for a more theological understanding of the Eucharist.

We can only be called to be saints in virtue of the perfect obedience of Christ in his perfect sacrifice of himself and the Father's acceptance of this offering in the glory of the resurrection. It is again, the mystery of his sacred humanity that points the way for us. As he willingly took upon himself the misery, suffering, and humiliation of the cross, we, too, in our own human lives now have a new principle by which to live our "life in Christ." In taking on a nature like ours in all things but sin, Jesus Christ imbued human nature with a new dignity and meaning. In the same way, in willingly taking on the suffering of his passion and death he gave new significance to all the suffering, misery, and humiliation of the baptized. The suffering and struggles of the priest now have salvific purpose in light of his conformity to Christ the High Priest and Suffering Servant.

THE EUCHARIST AND PRAYER

One of the lessons I learned early in my life as a priest is that, strange as it may seem, Mass is not enough. While daily celebration of the Eucharist is truly the priest's daily bread, a habit of personal prayer is required for discovering much of what has been given in the Mass. Prayer here is not the praying of the breviary, a serious sacerdotal obligation, nor the saying of prayers or even the reading of the scripture, *lectio divina*, if you will. Here I speak of a daily period of time, at least one half-hour, when we sit before God in silence and attempt to place ourselves at his disposal and to listen for his direction and word. It can

What is received in the Eucharist is explored in prayer.

be called meditation or mental prayer and can take as many forms as there are persons. Some traditions of spirituality such as Carmelites and Jesuits have their own formulas to guide the beginner.

Prayer is the raising of the mind and heart to God. It is also the attempt to present oneself to the Lord in receptivity of mind and heart, avoiding the obstacles to true spiritual attention such as distractions or our own material or spiritual agendas. Prayer requires the ability to wait on God and to endure long periods of aridity and the lack of consolation. In prayer one waits upon God in faith, trusting that he will send the Holy Spirit to pray within us. Prayer is the work of the Holy Spirit in much the same way as the sacraments are the work of the Holy Spirit. What is received in the Eucharist is explored in prayer, and the need to go forward is concretized and made real.

The graces of conversion and virtue, bestowed in the Eucharist, often require this time of reflection and openness to God for the concrete implications of these eucharistic gifts to be understood and made a part of daily life. The life of personal prayer flows from the Mass and prepares one to receive the Eucharist in greater purity of heart. Growth in the spiritual life, dependent as it is on the bread that comes down from heaven, is gradual and progressive. To stay close to Christ in the Eucharist is the great spiritual norm of priestly spirituality.

Many young priests, as young Catholics in general, find exposition of the Blessed Sacrament in the monstrance particularly helpful in developing a sound relationship with the eucharistic Lord. The phenomenon of adoration chapels in many parishes within the last decade or so is evidence of this strong eucharistic devotion. While no one suggests that Christ is more present in the exposed sacrament than in the tabernacle, this physical visibility can be a powerful aid in learning to be attentive to the Lord in prayer. The important truth that must not be lost is that exposition of the Blessed Sacrament is an extension of the Mass. It prolongs the Mass in much the same way as the Hours of the Divine Office extend the Eucharist throughout the day. It is not intended simply as another religious experience, but a means to drawing the adorer into a deeper life of prayer, a more intimate relationship with Christ. The daily holy hour, so common among the newly ordained, is the disciplined way in which priests attend to this need, even when exposition and adoration are not available.

Exposition of the Blessed Sacrament is an extension of the Mass.

In my formation, prayer before the Blessed Sacrament did not suggest exposition nor propose that as an ideal. We cannot be a Church without the Eucharist, and we cannot remain faithful as priests without the Eucharist. The daily celebration of the Mass and devotion to Christ continually present in the eucharistic species are essential, no matter what form they take.

Bring Us to Perfection

Because the sacraments are made up of material things, they address us as we are, enfleshed human beings, and they bring us into contact, into communion, with the spiritual, the divine. This has been a consolation to me over the years, especially in times of difficulty or discouragement. To know that Christ has provided the remedy for my inclination to live without reference to God, to become too occupied with matters that are passing and unimportant, encourages me and provides the incentive to rise above my selfish and petty concerns. I can confess my many sins to the priest and be forgiven; I can bring my ailing body to the Church for strength and healing; I can meet Christ in the Eucharist as loving me in spite of all that I lack in my human nature flawed by sin. It is that meeting with Jesus Christ in the sacraments that makes perseverance in the priesthood possible and a source of contentment and joy. In the Eucharist, Christ makes me free to truly serve others and to lead them to know him in the intimacy of love.

Meeting Jesus Christ in the sacraments makes perseverance in the priesthood possible and is a source of contentment and joy.

"O Sacred Banquet, in which Christ becomes our food, the memory of his passion is renewed and the soul is filled with grace"—this is the antiphon from the office of Corpus Christi, which the priest never tires of repeating. May the eucharistic Lord bring to perfection within us what he began at the moment of our ordination and First Mass.

GOD WAITS FOR ME
Rev. Msgr. Stephen J. Rossetti

Practically every day, for the past thirty years, I have spent an hour in prayer before the Blessed Sacrament. I first heard about the idea of a daily "holy hour" when I was a seminarian. I knew that this was something for me. So, each day I rise and spend an hour before the tabernacle, or at least in a quiet place if the Sacrament is not at hand.

Jesus waits for us in this sacrament of love.

—Dominicae Cenae 3

Some priests find the prospect of an hour of prayer each day to be daunting. However, the time flies by; I start—and suddenly it is over. I typically combine quiet meditation with a slow reading of the Liturgy of the Hours. In prayer, we enter into God's timelessness.

I began this holy hour as a way to nourish my spiritual life and to be more open to the Spirit. I strongly believe that my priesthood has become more fruitful because of this "investment." I do not think I would have enough time to do all that I need to do as a priest if I did not spend this hour in prayer.

But, in the last few years, my focus has changed. I have come to treasure this time simply to be with the Lord. I feel his presence and find it brings me a deep peace and joy. I look forward to being with him.

And now, after many years, I sense that it is he who longs for these daily encounters even more than I. Just as a loving parent longs for the return of a child, so our loving God waits for us. As I step into the chapel to begin the hour, I feel a sense of relief to be back "home" and to "see" his face. But more than I, it is he who has been waiting for me.

A Lover's Longing for Communion
Rev. George E. Stuart

———

A theology of the Eucharist is a theology of the body. Through the Eucharist we understand the incarnation of Jesus and the high regard in which our bodies must be held. The Son of God came to us in a body like ours, and it is in our resurrected bodies, glorified and perfected, that we will see our God "face to face." And this seeing will not be impassive looking at a distance, but as embracing our beloved.

> We can say not only that each of us receives Christ, but also that Christ receives each of us.
> —Ecclesia de Eucharistia 22

The Song of Songs is a dialogue of lovers. The Bride says to the Bridegroom, "O that you would kiss me with the kisses of your mouth! Wine cannot ravish the senses like your embrace" (Song 1:2, based on RSV and Knox). The Bride's desire for the Bridegroom is a joyful regard for the other in whom she finds her fulfillment. The Bridegroom responds to the Bride: "You have ravished my heart, my sister, my bride, you have ravished my heart with a glance of your eyes . . ." (Song 4:9).

The Bride longs for bodily union, for holy communion, with him who longs to unite with her as well. "I was sleeping," she says, "but my heart kept vigil; I heard my lover knocking: 'Open to me, my sister, my beloved, my dove, my perfect one!'" (Song 5:2).

We know that Christ is the Bridegroom and we, the Church, are his Bride. But we may ask precisely how do we become "one

143

flesh" with him? The Bridegroom comes to us under the appearance of bread and wine precisely so that we can receive him bodily. He desires this union as well, more than we can know.

A mediaeval theologian saw the plural "kisses" of the Bride and the Bridegroom as our Holy Communion, not given and received just once, but again and again. The Eucharist is the pledge, and Holy Communion the consummation, of our divine love.

> It is not the eucharistic food that is changed into us, but rather we who are mysteriously transformed by it. Christ nourishes us by uniting us to himself; "he draws us into himself."
> —*Sacramentum Caritatis* 70

Thanksgiving for God's Victory of Love
Cardinal Albert Vanhoye, S.J.

———

The Eucharist is an inexhaustible mystery because it makes present the whole of Christ's paschal mystery. It is understood in a multitude of aspects and inspires a multitude of spiritualities with different nuances, corresponding to the diverse situations and vocations of Christian men and women.

Priests who celebrate the Eucharist have the privilege of a special union with Jesus that is more intimate and stronger, and more demanding as well, from the very moment Jesus instituted it. Two aspects of this priestly eucharistic spirituality seem especially important to me: the attitude of opening up, in thanksgiving, to the outpouring of love that comes from God, and the offering of oneself for a victory of that love over evil and death.

These two aspects are closely interconnected because one cannot, in all circumstances, gain this victory of love unless one welcomes in thanksgiving, in all circumstances, the outpouring of love coming from God.

A Priestly Spirituality of Thanksgiving

As a priest celebrating the Eucharist, I have realized more and more the importance of thanksgiving. At the Last Supper, Jesus began by giving thanks. He took the bread and gave thanks; he took the cup and gave thanks. The Church has understood well the fundamental importance of this attitude of thanksgiving in naming the sacrament that Jesus instituted "Eucharist." *Eucharistia* is a Greek word that means *thanksgiving*.

At first sight, the thanksgiving of Jesus at the Last Supper was an ordinary prayer of everyday life—the prayer of thanks for the food and the drink that are gifts of God's paternal love. But, in reality, this ordinary prayer took an extraordinary depth, because it anticipated what Jesus said immediately afterward: "This is my body. . . . This is my blood." Thus he gave his body and his blood to his disciples.

For Jesus, the first characteristic of the Eucharist is that it is a gift of the Father.

His prayer meant: "I thank you, Father, to have given me my body, which I can transform into a spiritual food giving it to my disciples, to share with them the divine life. I thank you for having given me my blood, which I can transform into a spiritual drink giving it to my disciples, to share with them the love that comes from you. I thank you especially because you are now putting into my heart all the power of your love, which makes me capable of this complete gift of myself." For Jesus, in reality, the first characteristic of the Eucharist is that it is a gift of the Father.

After the miracle of the multiplication of the loaves, which was a sign of this gift, Jesus gave his discourse on the Bread of Life. In this discourse, he proclaimed the gift: "It was not Moses who gave you the bread from heaven; my Father gives you the true bread from heaven. For the bread of God is that which comes down from heaven and gives life to the world" (Jn 6:32–33). Jesus does not claim to have taken the initiative for this marvelous gift himself, but he gives thanks, in effect saying, "Father, I unite myself with you, full of an immense gratitude, because you make of me the living bread, which gives the life to the world, bread multiplied infinitely for the profit of all."

Priestly spirituality must thus be, before all else, a spirituality of thanksgiving which unites us to the heart of the Son, full of gratitude toward the Father. This is fundamental because, as St. John writes, "not that we have loved God, but that he loved us and sent his Son as expiation for our sins (1 Jn 4:10). "He first loved us" (1 Jn 4:19). Because we are self-focused and thus "full of ourselves," this attitude of thanksgiving is not something spontaneous in us. In one way or another, in our thoughts, concerns, and achievements, we often put ourselves in the first place.

Instead, the celebration of the Eucharist should teach us to thank God continuously and to put God in the first place. The Eucharistic Prayers are, before all else, prayers of thanksgiving. They are introduced by a liturgical dialogue where the celebrant invites the people: "Let us give thanks to the Lord our God," and the people answer: "It is right to give him thanks and praise." Then, the Eucharistic Prayer commences with a preface that sets the same orientation by saying to God: "Father, all-powerful and ever-living God, we do well always and everywhere to give you thanks."

Priestly spirituality must thus be, before all else, a spirituality of thanksgiving.

In celebrating the Eucharist, the priest, above all, must unite himself to Christ's thanksgiving, keeping this union "always and everywhere," in order to communicate it to the people of God. The life of the priest should be a witness and a continual invitation to the faithful to give thanks.

Paul, the apostle, enjoined Christians "to give thanks in all circumstances" (1 Thes 5:18). He told them to "give thanks at all times and for everything to God the Father in the name of Our Lord, Jesus Christ" (Eph 5:20). He himself gave us an example of this attitude, because he regularly began each of his letters with an expression of thanksgiving to God, most often using the Greek verb for Eucharist, "I give thanks" (1 Rom 1:8; 1 Cor 1:4; Phil 1:3; 1 Thes 1:2; 2 Thes 1:3; Phlm 1:4), and sometimes with the equivalent expression: "Blessed be God . . ." (2 Cor 1:3; Eph 1:3).

The grace of God is offered to us "in all circumstances," even and especially in the painful ones, that unite us to the passion of

Christ, source of all graces. It is right and good, therefore, "in all circumstances," to receive gratefully the graces offered to us.

We should not forget that it was in very painful circumstances that Jesus gave thanks. St. Paul tells us: "The Lord Jesus, on the night he was handed over, took bread, and, after he had given thanks, broke it . . ." (1 Cor 11:23–24). The gospels show us that Jesus had understood that he was betrayed by one of his apostles. He announced it: "Amen, I say to you, one of you will betray me" (Mt 26:21). The series of events that would lead to his condemnation and cruel death had already been set in motion. Jesus knew it. Nevertheless, he gave thanks, that is to say, he opened himself with gratitude to the outpouring of love that comes from the Father.

THE TOTAL VICTORY OF LOVE

It is here that the other aspect of the Eucharist I previously mentioned appears: the Eucharist, as an offering of oneself in view of love's victory over evil and death, a victory made possible by this attitude of thanksgiving.

The institution of the Eucharist on Holy Thursday was an extraordinary victory of love over all the forces of evil and death.

When one speaks of the Eucharist, one usually focuses on the marvelous intimacy it creates between the faithful and Jesus. "Whoever eats my flesh and drinks my blood remains in me and I in him" (Jn 6:56). This aspect of intimacy is indeed the gift of an amazing love. But to limit oneself to it loses much of the richness of the sacrament and especially of its dynamism. Priestly spirituality should be especially conscious of another aspect: the institution of the Eucharist on Holy Thursday was an extraordinary victory of love over all the forces of evil and death.

Jesus knew that his ministry and his generous devotion to the service of God and humanity would be interrupted brutally by treason, a sin most odious and most contrary to the dynamics of a relationship. He knew that he would be denied by Peter, abandoned by his other disciples, arrested like a criminal, accused by false witnesses, condemned with the greatest injustice, and executed. What was his reaction?

What would be the reaction one could expect in such a scandalous situation? There are close similarities between Jesus' situation and that of Jeremiah. Like Jeremiah, Jesus was aware that he lived in a time of terrible crisis for his people. Like Jeremiah, Jesus predicted the destruction of the Temple of Jerusalem. Let us see the reaction of the prophet Jeremiah. Warned by God of a plot against him, Jeremiah exclaimed, "But, you, O Lord of hosts, O just Judge, searcher of mind and heart, Let me witness the vengeance you take on them, for to you I have entrusted my cause!" This petition can be read twice in the Book of Jeremiah, in 12:20 and 20:12. In a third passage, the prophet specifies what the divine revenge should be: "Heed me, O Lord, and listen to what my adversaries say. . . . So now, deliver their children to famine, do away with them by the sword. Let their wives be made childless and widows; let their men die of pestilence, their young men be slain by the sword in battle. . . . Forgive not their crime" (Jer 18:19, 21, 23).

In so cruel a situation of injustice, one can understand Jeremiah's behavior. However, one could add that Jeremiah's attitude is already some progress from the instinctive human reaction to take weapons in one's

> What more could Jesus have done for us? Truly, in the Eucharist, he shows us a love which goes "to the end," a love which knows no measure.
> —*Ecclesia de Eucharistia* 25

own hands and take revenge by oneself. Jeremiah entrusts his cause to God. He leaves it to God to do justice, which is already a victory over the impulse to do justice by oneself.

But Jesus gains a much more radical and positive victory, namely the total victory of love. Jesus, at the Last Supper, overcomes his deep sadness; he was "deeply troubled" (Jn 13:21), and instead of giving up his attitude of generosity, as did Jeremiah, he carries it to the extreme: "He loved his own in the world and he loved them to the end" (Jn 13:1), even giving up his life for them: "No one has greater love than this" (Jn 15:13).

Jesus anticipates his own death, and transforms it into a gift of love. He makes this gift present in advance in the bread broken, which becomes his body, and in the wine poured out, which becomes his blood. Thus, he gives himself to his disciples.

It is not possible to imagine a greater generosity than this, a gift of love more total, a more complete victory of love over evil and death, nor to imagine a more radical transformation of what happened. Because in instituting the Eucharist, Jesus not only transformed the bread into his body and the wine in his blood, he transformed, at the same time, the event itself— what happened at his passion and death.

> He desires to communicate to his disciples his own admiration and gratitude for all that he receives from the Father. He lives in thanksgiving and influences his disciples to do the same.
> —*The Eucharist, Gift of Divine Life*[34]

It seems to me that we are not attentive enough to this transformation, which is of no less importance than the transubstantiation. In a certain sense, one can say that it is even more important for our lives, because it communicates to us the dynamism of victorious love.

JESUS' EXTRAORDINARY TRANSFORMATION OF DEATH

At the Last Supper, Jesus transformed the event of a rupture of relations between persons into a means of establishing new relations with God and humanity in a perfect communion. He made of his blood, criminally spilled by his enemies, a blood of alliance, to the profit of all.

In the Old Testament, death was a radical break with others and with God. Now, because Jesus at the Last Supper changed the meaning of death, we can no longer consider death in this completely negative way. Death still breaks the physical bonds between people. It is no longer possible to communicate with somebody who is dead. It serves no purpose to speak to a dead person. One can no longer have a reciprocal relationship. This makes us feel sad. But now we know that not all the bonds are broken. In Christ, we remain spiritually united with those who have died.

In the Old Testament, the rupture caused by death seemed total, especially for our relationship with God. Death, the punishment for sin and the ultimate consequence of sin, caused a complete separation from God. Between the corruption of death and the holiness of God, there does not appear to be any possibility of a relationship. It appeared that God no longer remembers the dead. "You remember them no more; they are cut off from your care" (Ps 88:6), and the dead, for their part, cannot rise to praise God (Is 38:18). The rupture caused by death became even more tragic in the case of someone condemned to death, rejected, and cursed.

The institution of the Eucharist was thus an extraordinary victory of love over the sins of humanity and death.

It is this dreadful rupture that Jesus had to face. St. Paul did not hesitate to say that Jesus became a curse for us, for it is written, "Cursed be everyone who hangs on a tree," (Gal 3:13; Dt 21:23). At the Last Supper, Jesus faced this situation in advance and he made of it an occasion of the greatest love, an instrument of communion with God and humanity—with God in filial obedience, with humanity in fraternal solidarity. The institution of the Eucharist was thus an extraordinary victory of love over the sins of humanity and death.

It seems to me that we do not realize sufficiently the extraordinary transformation accomplished by Jesus at that moment, or the generosity of his heart when conceiving and winning this victory of love. We do not realize sufficiently the dynamism of the victorious love that Christ wants to share with us when we celebrate the Eucharist and receive communion. This dynamism should make easy the victory over all our obstacles to love, and it should give us the power to transform these same obstacles into occasions to grow in love. Celebrating the Eucharist, I have become aware that as a priest associated more directly to what Jesus accomplished at the Last Supper, I am called to generously live in my life this victory of love, the victory of the Good Shepherd, who "lays down his life for his sheep" (Jn 10:11).

As a priest, I am called to generously live in my life this victory of love.

The institution of the Eucharist radically renewed the idea of sacrifice. The sacrifice of Christ at the Last Supper consisted—let us repeat it—in putting himself at the service of the love, which came to him from the Father, to gain the victory of love over evil and death. Christ received this love with thanksgiving.

SPREADING THE FIRE OF LOVE

When we celebrate the Eucharist, we are invited to receive, with thanksgiving, this divine love that comes to us through Jesus, and then to place ourselves at the service of this love for our entire lives, for its continuous victory. In the old sacrifices, the fire of the furnace had a decisive function: it is this that brought about the sacrificial transformation and made the offering pass into the divine sphere. In the Christian sacrifice, the fire of the furnace is replaced by the fire of the divine love that wants to be spread throughout our entire existence for our sanctification and for the transformation of the world.

As a priest, I am asked to receive in the Eucharist this fire of love, this fire of the Holy Spirit, to be able to communicate it as St. Paul did. Thus, he defined priestly spirituality: "to carry out my priestly duty by bringing the gospel of God to the Gentiles, and to make them acceptable as an offering, sanctified by the Holy Spirit" (Rom 15:16).

Christ gives the dignity of a royal priesthood to the people he has made his own. From these, with a brother's love, he chooses men to share his sacred ministry by the laying on of hands. He appoints them to renew in his name the sacrifice of our redemption as they set before your family his paschal meal.
—Preface of the Chrism Mass

What You Receive as a Gift, Give as a Gift
Rev. Edward J. Arsenault

———

In Matthew 10, Jesus sends out the Twelve to continue his work. Issuing his mandate, the Lord reminds them that they are to give freely what they have received as a gift.

As one who presides at the Eucharist, different aspects of each Eucharistic Prayer have stood out for me at different times. Most recently, a beautiful passage from the Eucharistic Prayer III struck me, "Lord, may this sacrifice, which has made our peace with you, advance the peace and salvation of all the world."

The first gift that flows from Christ's sacrifice is his peace. How at peace am I with being the unmerited recipient of this sacrifice and this gift of salvation? I should live in a spirit of thanksgiving for so great a gift. This prayer also challenges me to live in peace with others, especially those with whom I differ or whom I may even oppose.

Finally, and perhaps most poignantly, I ponder how well I see the mission of the Church as advancing "the peace and salvation of all the world." The worthy evangelist is driven by a confident faith that God's peace is already ours and is offered to all as well. Such passion stands at the heart of the Church's mission to "tell the Good News."

I recently met a woman who was struggling with finding peace in her life. We both came to realize that, at root of her lack of peace with others, was a lack of peace within herself as beloved of God. Once she embraced God's love for her, she came to see how she could love others in the same way. In receiving God's peace, she became his ambassador as well.

The relationship between the Eucharistic mystery and social commitment must be made explicit.
—Sacramentum Caritatis 89

May our experience of God's love for us, made real at the eucharistic table, inspire us to be icons and ambassadors of Christ's peace. What you receive as a gift, give as a gift.

GO AND LIVE THE MASS!
Rev. Msgr. Peter J. Vaghi

———

In my twenty-fourth year of priesthood, I have come to appreciate how the words of the dismissal seem to permeate the entire Mass for me. In Latin, the command is: *Ite, Missa est.* Simply translated, it means "Go, the Mass is." The Mass never ends; it continues always. These words highlight that the liturgy is directed not only to the Mystery we encounter in the sacred species, but also the assurance that this encounter changes us and guides us daily once the liturgy is over. We ourselves, by the grace and transforming power of this Holy Sacrament, are challenged to be taken, blessed, broken, and given, in effect, to put into action in our daily lives, the Love we have just celebrated.

To understand more deeply the implications of this challenging dismissal of the Mass, I ask you to go with me to the Upper Room. I invite you to focus on Jesus' words there as he washed his apostles' feet: "If I, therefore, the master and teacher, have washed your feet, you ought to wash one another's feet" (Jn 13:14). This humble action of Jesus, and the words he uttered there about love and service, help us understand what it means to follow the command to live the Mass.

I am constantly amazed at the incredible generosity of so many followers of Jesus. There is a direct link to the frequent feasting on the body and blood of Jesus at Mass and the work of Christian service. I think of so many of my friends and parishioners who, for example, donate precious time in pro-bono legal and medical work, those who clean the bedpans of people too sick to help themselves, and those who donate time in our parishes and other institutions of service. These are all ways of "washing feet," of living the eucharistic love that transforms us at Mass. In the words of Father Jean Galot in his book *The Eucharistic Heart*:

> From then on, the Eucharist has contained within itself the power of humble love which led to the washing of the feet. . . . Those who receive the body of the Lord and who open themselves to its spiritual influence, are transformed by it in such a way that they adopt the attitude of service and humble devotedness that inspired the institution of the Eucharist.[35]

Thus, Jesus' example of humble service and love is more than just a model. In the Eucharist the strength to imitate his life and to follow the missionary command, "Go, live the Mass," are communicated to us. The eucharistic food assimilates us, transforms us, and introduces us into a higher life. Model and power all in one! Go and live! Service to the poor, witness to charity, the defense and promotion of every person's life from conception to natural death, the struggle for justice and the constant search for peace flow from and are developed and sustained by the eucharistic mystery.

This celebration, if it is to be genuine and complete, should lead to various works of charity . . . as well as . . . to different forms of Christian witness.
—Presbyterorum Ordinis 6

The daily celebration of the Mass, which priests are privileged to celebrate, prepares us for life beyond the Mass. The challenge is to understand that deep mystery and live it. How then can the dismissal, so understood, not permeate our understanding of all we do at the altar of the Lord? *Ite Missa est!* Go live the Mass!

After the blessing, the deacon or the priest dismisses the people with the words: *Ite, missa est.* These words help us to grasp the relationship between the Mass just celebrated and the mission of Christians in the world. . . . The word "dismissal" has come to imply a "mission." . . . The People of God might be helped to understand more clearly this essential dimension of the Church's life, taking the dismissal as a starting-point.
—*Sacramentum Caritatis* 51

CONCLUSION
Rev. Msgr. Stephen J. Rossetti

———

PRIESTLY IDENTITY IN THE EUCHARIST

In this book, Fr. Gabriel O'Donnell spoke of a new current in the Church, that is, a renewed devotion to the Eucharist. He has witnessed "fervent young men and women today who are decidedly more eucharistic in their attachment to exposition of the Blessed Sacrament, holy hours, and new forms of eucharistic devotion. All this is in addition to attendance at daily Mass." I, too, have seen perpetual adoration spring up in parishes around the country and faithfully served by lay parishioners who regularly spend hours in eucharistic devotion. I find this astounding and encouraging.

> *I would like to rekindle this Eucharistic "amazement."*
> —Ecclesia de Eucharistia 6

So, too, among many priests, does there seem to be a resurgence of love and reverence for the Sacrifice of the Mass and for the eucharistic Christ. In the days after the Vatican Council, it became common to hear of an identity crisis in the priesthood. As the laity began to take on a more active role in the Church, as indeed they should and are called to do, this became unsettling for some and a source of disorientation. What was the role and identity of the priest?

In this book, it has become clear from where the source of our priestly identity springs. In his chapter, Archbishop Wuerl wrote: "Often, we hear the question: Is there a distinct spirituality of the diocesan priest? . . . The answer is found in our grasp of the ministry of the priest, which is so intimately tied to the sacraments and particularly the celebration of the Eucharist . . . This is both our ministry and our identity." In his chapter, Cardinal Dulles's words echoed the same thought. Quoting John Paul II, he wrote, "The Eucharist . . . is the *raison d'être* of the priesthood."

If there had been a crisis of identity of the priesthood in previous years, it necessarily must have been accompanied by a weakened understanding of the Eucharist and the priest's connection to it. *As we lose a sense of the Eucharist, we lose a sense of the priesthood. As we fail to recognize Christ present in the Eucharist, we fail to recognize Christ uniquely present in the priest.*

How can there be an identity crisis when the true nature of the Eucharist is known? How can there be a lack of vocations to the priesthood, when its true greatness is understood? We, priests, are abundantly blessed to have been called to such a life. And we do a great service to young men around the world

> Priestly piety, nourished at the table of God's Word and the Holy Eucharist, lived within the cycle of the liturgical year, inspired by a warm and enlightened devotion to the Virgin Mother of the Supreme and Eternal High Priest and Queen of the Apostles, will bring him to the source of a true spiritual life which alone provides a solid foundation for the observance of celibacy.
> —*Sacerdotalis Caelibatus* 75

when we invite them to discern a priestly calling. I suspect that we will find an upsurge in priestly vocations, particularly in those places where a devotion to the Eucharist is fostered. I have seen signs of this already.

EUCHARISTIC WONDER

When Pope John Paul II wrote *Ecclesia de Eucharistia*, he said his purpose was to rekindle a sense of "eucharistic amazement." In *Sacramentum Caritatis*, Pope Benedict XVI prayed that the Holy Spirit would enkindle in us a "eucharistic wonder." Amazement and wonder are two apt words to describe the Eucharist and thus the calling of the priest.

I personally have been blessed to have been engaged in this book on the priesthood and the Eucharist. Meditating on the words of these authors, searching more deeply into the teaching of the Church, and spending time in prayer before the Blessed Sacrament asking for help, I believe I have moved one step deeper into the mystery of the Eucharist. It has been a most fruitful journey for me. My celebration of the Eucharist has been changed . . . enriched, deepened. I hope it does the same for you.

The ministerial priesthood . . . is born, lives, works and bears fruit de Eucharistia.
—John Paul II, Holy Thursday Letter, 2004

In my last book, I spoke of the importance of a devotion to the Blessed Virgin Mary, particularly for priests.[36] She is the Mother of all, but especially the Mother of priests. And when she looks upon us, she loves us with a special love because it is the face of her Son that she sees. She will never abandon us, just as she stayed close to her Son, even during his most painful hour on Calvary.

I have noticed over the years that the great saints typically have had a fervent devotion to Mary and a devotion to the eucharistic Christ. Many spent hours in front of the tabernacle in prayer, such as the great Curé of Ars. Many saints died with the names of Jesus and Mary on their lips. And they received the Eucharist at Mass with reverence and joy.

I chose the authors of these two books, the book on Mary and the book on the Eucharist, because of their unique gifts and because I thought they were exemplary priests. The inspiring words they have shared with us have confirmed the choices. We ought to emulate them in our devotion to Mary and to the eucharistic

Christ. We, too, aspire to mount the heights of sanctity, despite an awareness of our weakness and sin. But it is not in ourselves that we trust, but in him.

We have been given great gifts to guide us on our way. We have been given a beautiful Mother who is the model of all motherhood. She will not abandon us when our hour comes, just as she did not abandon her Son. And we have been given heavenly food for the journey, the eucharistic Christ feeds us with his divine life. How can we stray for long with such powerful aids?

Recently, during the year of my twenty-fifth anniversary of ordination, a pious layman said to me, "Father, I respect priests, especially because they have given up so much." I honestly said in reply, "I really do not feel like I have given up anything. I feel very fortunate." There is sacrifice to our life, as there is to any life on this earth. But we have been given a great treasure. As Pope Benedict wrote, "For in the most blessed Eucharist is contained the entire spiritual wealth of the Church, namely Christ himself" (*S Car* 16).

It is my hope that this book will enable each of us to plumb more deeply the unfathomable riches of the Eucharist. I hope that priests will come to appreciate more fully their identity with and in the Eucharist. You and I are born *de Eucharistia*. We are men of the Eucharist. And in this truth lies the majesty and joy of our calling.

Let this reflection end by joining in the prayer of our Holy Father at the end of his great apostolic exhortation on the Eucharist, *Sacramentum Caritatis*:

> Through the intercession of the Blessed Virgin Mary, may the Holy Spirit kindle within us the same ardour experienced by the disciples on the way to Emmaus and renew our "eucharistic wonder." (*S Car* 97)

ABBREVIATIONS

CCC:Catechism of the Catholic Church, United States Conference of Catholic Bishops, 1997.

DC: Dominicae Cenae (The Lord's Supper), John Paul II, Apostolic Letter, 1980.

DD: Dies Domini (On the Day of the Lord), John Paul II, Apostolic Letter, 1998.

DS: Denzinger-Schonmetzer, *Enchiridion Symbolorum*, Barcinone: Herder, 1965.

DV: Dei Verbum (Dogmatic Constitution on Divine Revelation), Vatican Council II, 1965.

EE: Ecclesia de Eucharistia (Church of the Eucharist), John Paul II, Encyclical Letter, 2003.

GIRM: "General Instruction on the Roman Missal," United States Conference of Catholic Bishops, 2003.

PD: Pastores Dabo Vobis (I Will Give You Shepherds), John Paul II, Post-Synodal Apostolic Exhortation, 1992.

SC: Sacrosanctum Concilium (Dogmatic Constitution on the Sacred Liturgy), Vatican Council II, 1963.

S Car: Sacramentum Caritatis (Sacrament of Charity), Benedict XVI, Post-Synodal Apostolic Exhortation, 2007.

PO: Presbyterorum Ordinis (Decree on the Ministry and Life of Priests), Vatican Council II, 1965.

The papal and conciliar documents cited above can be found on the Vatican website: www.vatican.va. Use the Latin name when searching for them. General audiences, homilies, etc., by the pope can also be found on the Vatican website. Search by the date of the address.

CONTRIBUTORS

Rev. Edward J. Arsenault is a priest of the Diocese of Manchester, New Hampshire. Ordained in 1991, Fr. Arsenault has served in parish ministry, Catholic health care ministry, and recently concluded ten years of service as moderator of the curia and vicar for administration. In October, 2009, Fr. Arsenault became president and CEO of Saint Luke Institute in Silver Spring, Maryland.

Rev. Timothy A. Butler, U.S.A.F., is a priest of the Archdiocese of Boston. He was ordained in 1988 and after serving as a parish priest for five years became a chaplain in the U.S. Air Force where he holds the rank of Lieutenant Colonel.

Rev. Daniel P. Coughlin was ordained for the Archdiocese of Chicago in 1960. He served in several parishes, as the first director of the Office for Divine Worship, and as vicar for priests until he became Chaplain of the U.S. House of Representatives in 2000.

Rev. Brendan Daly was ordained in 1977. He is principal of Good Shepherd College in Auckland, New Zealand and Associate Judicial Vicar of the Regional Tribunal of the Catholic Church for New Zealand.

Archbishop Timothy M. Dolan was named archbishop of New York in 2009. Ordained a priest in 1976 for the Archdiocese of St. Louis, he became an auxiliary bishop there in 2001. He was made archbishop of Milwaukee in 2002 where he served for seven years.

Cardinal Avery Dulles, S.J., an internationally known theologian, author, and lecturer, was born in 1918 in Auburn, New York to John Foster Dulles and Janet Pomeroy Avery Dulles. While a student at Harvard University, he converted to Catholicism, a journey which he related in the book *A Testimonial to Grace*. After serving in the Navy, he joined the Society of Jesus and was ordained to the priesthood in 1956. He received a doctorate in Sacred Theology from the Gregorian University in Rome and held a number

167

of faculty positions in theology. In his last assignment, he was the Laurence J. McGinley Professor of Religion and Society at Fordham University. He is the author of over seven hundred articles and twenty-two books, including the well known *Models of the Church*. The first U.S. theologian to be named to the College of Cardinals, he passed away on December 12, 2008.

Most Rev. Victor B. Galeone was ordained the ninth bishop of the Diocese of St. Augustine in 2001. Prior to that, he served as parochial vicar and pastor in the Archdiocese of Baltimore, and as a missionary in Peru for eleven years.

Cardinal Francis George, O.M.I., was installed as archbishop of Chicago in 1997. Prior to that he was archbishop of Portland, Oregon and Bishop of Yakima, Washington. He currently serves as President of the United States Conference of Catholic Bishops.

Rev. Benedict J. Groeschel, C.F.R., renowned author and spiritual director, is director of the Office for Spiritual Development of the Archdiocese of New York. He has worked with priests as a retreat leader and spiritual director for more than thirty years.

Rev. Msgr. Paul A. Lenz, a priest of the Diocese of Altoona-Johnstown, was ordained April 2, 1949. He has served as a pastor, university instructor, a missionary in Paraguay, director of the Society for the Propagation of the Faith, and as national director of Black and Indian Mission Office in Washington, D.C.

Cardinal Carlo Maria Martini, S.J., entered the Society of Jesus in 1944, was ordained a priest in 1972, a bishop in 1980, and created a cardinal in 1983. He was rector of the Pontifical Biblical Institute, rector of the Gregorian University, and archbishop of Milan from 1980 to 2002.

Most Rev. John B. McCormack is the bishop of Manchester, New Hampshire. He was ordained a priest in the Archdiocese of Boston in 1960 and made auxiliary bishop there in 1995.

Rev. Kevin M. McDonough was ordained for the Archdiocese of Saint Paul and Minneapolis in 1980. He has served as a seminary rector, vicar general, moderator of the curia, and is currently pastor of two parishes, one African-American and the other Hispanic.

Rev. **Peter Murphy** was ordained in 1970 in Auckland, New Zealand. He served in a number of parishes and is the national co-ordinator for the New Zealand Community for Christian Meditation.

Rev. **Gabriel B. O'Donnell, O.P.**, is a Dominican friar of the Eastern Province of Saint Joseph and currently serving as academic dean at the Pontifical Faculty of the Immaculate Conception at the Dominican House of Studies. He is also the vice-postulator for the cause for canonization of Venerable Father Michael J. McGivney, founder of the Knights of Columbus, and postulator for the cause of Rose Hawthorne, founder of the Dominican Sisters of Hawthorne, New York.

Rev. **Anthony Oelrich**, ordained in 1992, is the rector of St. Mary's Cathedral and pastor of St. Augustine's and Christ Church Newman Center in St. Cloud, Minnesota. He is also the director of continuing education for clergy for the Diocese of St. Cloud.

Rev. **Msgr. J. Wilfrid Parent** was ordained in 1991 for the Archdiocese of Washington. He has served as a pastor, parochial vicar, vice rector of Mount St. Mary's Seminary, and director of priestly vocations.

Rev. **George E. Stuart** was ordained a priest of the Archdiocese of Washington in 1989. He has served in various parishes and is now vice chancellor and archivist of the Archdiocese.

Rev. **Msgr. John J. Strynkowski** was ordained a priest for the Diocese of Brooklyn in 1963. He has served as a parochial vicar, official of the Vatican's Secretariat of State and the Congregation for Bishops, professor of theology and rector at the Seminary of the Immaculate Conception in Huntington, New York, pastor, and executive director of the Secretariat for Doctrine and Pastoral Practices at the United States Conference of Catholic Bishops. He is currently rector of St. James Cathedral Basilica in Brooklyn and vicar for higher education.

Rev. **David L. Toups**, ordained in 1997, is a priest of the Diocese of St. Petersburg in Florida. Currently the associate director of the Secretariat of Clergy, Consecrated Life, and Vocations at the United States Conference of Catholic Bishops, he has also served as parochial vicar, seminary professor, and dean of students at St. Vincent de Paul Regional Seminary in Boynton Beach, Florida.

Rev. Msgr. Peter J. Vaghi, a priest of the Archdiocese of Washington, is pastor of Little Flower Parish in Bethesda, Maryland. He has served in a number of parishes and is also chaplain to the John Carroll Society. Prior to his seminary studies he practiced law and remains a member of the Virginia and Washington, D.C., bars.

Cardinal Albert Vanhoye, S.J., entered the Jesuits in 1941, was ordained a priest in 1954, and was made a cardinal in 2006. He began his teaching ministry in France. He was then appointed professor at the Pontifical Biblical Institute in 1962 where he served as dean of the biblical faculty, director of the journal *Biblica*, and then rector. He was a member of the Pontifical Biblical Commission from 1984 to 2001.

Rev. Kevin Walsh, O.C.S.O., was ordained a diocesan priest in 1978. After various pastoral assignments he entered the Trappists in 2000 and professed solemn vows as a monk of Mepkin Abbey in 2006.

Rev. Stephen Wang is a priest of the Diocese of Westminster, England. He has been an associate pastor and university chaplain, and currently teaches philosophy and theology at Allen Hall, the seminary of the Archdiocese of Westminster.

Archbishop Donald W. Wuerl was installed in June 2006 as the sixth archbishop of Washington. He serves on numerous national and international bodies and is chairman of the United States Conference of Catholic Bishops' Committee on Evangelization and Catechesis. He has served as chairman of the U.S.C.C.B. committees on Education, Priestly Life and Ministry, the North American College, and Priestly Formation. He is the author of numerous articles and books, including *The Catholic Priesthood Today* and the best-selling catechisms, *The Teaching of Christ* and *The Catholic Way*.

Rev. Msgr. John Zenz was ordained in 1978 for the Archdiocese of Detroit and has served as an associate pastor, seminary professor and spiritual director, director of religious education for the archdiocese, chancellor, moderator of the curia and vicar general. Currently he serves as pastor of Holy Name Parish in Birmingham and is episcopal vicar for approximately seventy-five parishes of the Archdiocese.

NOTES

General audiences, addresses, etc., by the Pope and statements from offices and secretaries of the curia referred to in the text can be found on the Vatican website. Search by the date.

1. John Paul II, *Gift and Mystery* (New York: Doubleday, 1997), 77–78.
2. John Paul II, Talk at the American Cardinals Summit, Rome, April 23, 2002.
3. John Paul II, Address to the U.S. Bishops of Boston and Hartford, September 2, 2004, citing *Optatam Totius*, no. 1.
4. St. John Vianney, quoted in *Sacerdotii Nostri Primordia*, Encyclical Letter of Pope John XXIII, August 1, 1959.
5. *L'Osservatore Romano*, May 19, 1993.
6. John Paul II, *Gift and Mystery*, 77-78.
7. *The Pope Speaks*, 29:198.
8. Editor's note: The indult was not extended and the current "General Instruction of the Roman Missal" requires sacred vessels to be purified by the priest, deacon, or instituted acolyte.
9. John Paul II, General Audience, June 9, 1993.
10. *The Pope Speaks*, 29:198.
11. Cardinal Cláudio Hummes, Congregation for the Clergy, "Letter on the Occasion of the World Day of Prayer for the Sanctification of Priests," May 30, 2008.
12. John Paul II, General Audience, June 9, 1993.
13. Cardinal Gabriele M. Garron, Congregation for Catholic Education, "Spiritual Formation in Seminaries," January 6, 1980.
14. Joseph M. Champlin, *The Mystery and Meaning of the Mass* (New York: Crossroad 1999), 71.
15. Cardinal Cláudio Hummes, May 30, 2008.
16. John Paul II, June 9, 1993.
17. Joseph Ratzinger, *Called to Communion* (San Francisco: Ignatius Press, 1996), 32.

18. The section titles come from the Litany of the Most Blessed Sacrament.

19. The DVD *Fishers of Men* is an eighteen-minute promotional video on the priesthood produced by the United States Conference of Catholic Bishops' Secretariat of Clergy, Consecrated Life and Vocations (cf. www.usccb.org/cclv).

20. John Paul II, *Gift and Mystery*.

21. Benedict XVI, "Address to the Pontifical Ecclesiastical Academy," 9 June 2008 (*L'Osservatore Romano*, 18 June, 2008), 4.

22. St. Augustine's words in Latin are, "*O Sacramentum Pietatis! O Signum Unitatis! O Vinculum Caritatis!*" Tractates on the Gospel of John, Tract 26, 13.

23. Cf. Dean R. Hoge and Jacqueline E. Wenger, *Evolving Visions of the Priesthood: Changes from Vatican II to the Turn of the New Century* (Collegeville: Liturgical Press, 2003), 114.

24. Celebrating alone is not the ideal, but when need be, there is such value in the gift of the celebration of the Eucharist that the priest should not fail to offer it for the needs of his people and indeed of the whole world. Contrary to what some may say, the Church highly encourages the practice of the *missa sine populo*. Relying upon the texts of Vatican II, Pope John Paul II wrote: "If the priest 'hears' this truth proposed to him and to all of the faithful as the voice of the New Testament and Tradition, he will grasp the Council's earnest recommendation of the 'daily celebration (of the Eucharist), which is an act of Christ and the Church even if it is impossible for the faithful to be present' [*Presbyterorum Ordinis*, 13]. The tendency to celebrate the Eucharist only when there was an assembly of the faithful emerged in those years [after Vatican II]. According to the Council, although everything possible should be done to gather the faithful for the celebration, it is also true that, even if the priest is alone, the eucharistic offering that he performs in the name of Christ has the effectiveness that comes from Christ and always obtains new graces for the Church. Therefore, I too recommend to priests and to all the Christian people that they ask the Lord for a stronger faith in this value of the Eucharist" (*Priesthood in the Third Millennium: Addresses of Pope John Paul II, 1993*, ed. James P. Socias [Princeton:

Scepter Publishers, 1994]), 65. Cf. also the *Code of Canon Law*, 904 and *Ecclesia de Eucharistia*, 31.

25. Archbishop Fulton J. Sheen, *Treasure in Clay* (San Francisco: Ignatius Press, 1993), 190-191.

26. Benedict XVI, "Address to Priests of the Archdiocese of Brindisi," 15 June 2008 (*L'Osservatore Romano*, 18 June 2008), 9.

27. Benedict XVI, "Fostering 'Obedience to the Truth,'" (*L'Osservatore Romano*, 18 October 2006), 4.

28. St. Francis de Sales, quoted in John P. McClernon, editor, *Sermon in a Sentence: A Treasury of Quotations on the Spiritual Life*, vol. 2: St. Francis de Sales (San Francisco: Ignatius Press, 2003), 166.

29. St. Alphonsus Liguori, ed. by Charles Dollen, *The Holy Eucharist* (New York: Alba House, 1999), 58.

30. Ibid, 22.

31. Jean Galot S.J., *The Eucharistic Heart*, (Dublin: Veritas, 1990), 61.

32. The Theological-Historical Commission for the Great Jubilee of the Year 2000, trans. by Robert R. Barr, *The Eucharist, Gift of Divine Life* (New York: Crossroad, 1999), 98.

33. Galot, 30.

34. The Theological-Historical Commission, 56.

35. Galot, 61.

36. *Behold Your Mother: Priests Speak about Mary* (Notre Dame, IN: Ave Maria Press, 2007).

MSGR. STEPHEN J. ROSSETTI served as president and CEO of Saint Luke Institute in Silver Spring, Maryland from 1997 until October of 2009, and for three years prior to that as a staff member. A priest of the Diocese of Syracuse, he previously served in two diocesan parishes. He is a licensed psychologist with a PhD in psychology from Boston College and a Doctor of Ministry from the Catholic University of America. He is the author of scores of articles and several books including *The Joy of Priesthood*—recipient of a Catholic Press Association book award (Ave Maria Press, 2005), *When the Lion Roars* (Ave Maria Press, 2003), and editor of *Behold Your Mother* (Ave Maria Press, 2007). Msgr. Rossetti has received a Proclaim Award from the USCCB as well as a Lifetime Service Award from the Theological College of the Catholic University of America. He lectures to priests and religious internationally on priestly spirituality and wellness issues. In January of 2010 he will join the theological faculty of the Catholic University of America.

Founded in 1865, Ave Maria Press,
a ministry of the Congregation of
Holy Cross, is a Catholic publishing
company that serves the spiritual and
formative needs of the Church and its
schools, institutions, and ministers;
Christian individuals and families; and
others seeking spiritual nourishment.

For a complete listing of titles from

Ave Maria Press

Sorin Books

Forest of Peace

Christian Classics

visit www.avemariapress.com

ave maria press / Notre Dame, IN 46556
A Ministry of the Indiana Province of Holy Cross